From Grief
to Gladness

Coming Back
from Widowhood

BY

JANE GRIZ JONES

RECOVERY COMMUNICATIONS, INC.
P.O. Box 19910, Baltimore, Maryland 21211 • (410) 243-8558

Please visit our website at http://www.Recovery Communications.com
for books and free reports about recovery and the joy of living,
and for a free e-mail subscription to the Getting Them Sober newsletter.

With a few exceptions, the names of persons other than myself who figure in this account have been purposely changed, although most of those who played a part in my story would be more than willing to be known by name.

The exceptions are my late husband, Paul Griz, my children, and my present husband, Boyce Jones.

Boyce is my ever-present helper and my best friend, and I rejoice that God sent me this wonderful companion to go with me the rest of the way.

ISBN 1-891874-06-3

Dedication

In loving memory
of
Paul Griz
and
June Jones

Table of Contents

Acknowledgments

This book only happened because of the dear friends who never stopped encouraging me to write my story, the many senior adults who have shared their love and my ministry with me, and the other "merry widows" who endured with me through the tears and helped me rediscover the joys of laughter.

Special thanks to Betsy Tice White, my editor and friend, for her tireless efforts in bringing this book to reality. She is another one of my "special angels."

Foreword

Bob Norman, Pastor Emeritus
Clearview Baptist Church
Franklin, Tennessee

Every life has its many-colored patches — its exciting thrills, its surges of wild emotion, its golden dreams, its excruciating heartbreak, and its floods of tears. When all the facts are known, many persons we had thought were trouble-free are found to be carrying around in their hearts things we would not wish to take on.

After a happy togetherness of 33 years, "Paul's wife" became a widow as a consequence of her husband's malignant melanoma. Stunned by the suddenness of the death of Paul Griz, over the next 13 years Jane learned that God will mend a broken heart — but only if you give Him all the pieces.

Death is something we all must ultimately expect, but when the one who dies is a beloved companion, the loss is an acute and desperate one, a sorrow that softens only with time. And the memories are never completely erased. Asking God "Why?" is all right. Jane Griz had to face that question before she could work through her sorrow.

As she tells her story, the process of doing the grief work is included all the way from handling the holidays through letting go, visiting her husband's grave, and even whether to continue wearing her wedding ring. With the passing of time the reality of her husband's death began to sink deeper into her soul. "When" is important in everything, on both the light and the serious sides of life. Many centuries ago it was said, "To everything there is a season, and a time to every purpose under heaven."

There always have been and always will be things we cannot foresee, things of which we are afraid. Yet we must not let the certainty of uncertainty prevent us from reaching out for constructive plans and purposes. We lived through yesterday, and with faith we will face the challenges of tomorrow. There is always a future, and we know that providential purposes do prevail.

From Grief to Gladness encourages readers to live life as it goes on, rather than as if all were over. I tip my hat to Jane Griz Jones for her honest insight into the tragic Fridays, gloomy Saturdays, and victorious Sunday mornings of life. You will see the whole of life as a grander, holier thing once you have read this memorable book.

*"The Lord will fulfill His
purpose for me; Your love,
O Lord, endures forever.
Do not abandon the works of
your hands."*

— Psalm 138, verse 8 (NIV)

Part One

A Plight

Many books and articles have been written about how we are to deal with our grief. Yet the situation is different for every one of the millions of women and men of all ages who are suddenly left, as I was, with a broken heart.

Perhaps you are recently widowed, or a widow or widower of long standing, grasping for something that can give you hope, some reason to go on living. Believe me, I have been exactly where you are now, and as I tell you my story, I am praying for you to receive the strong knowledge that better days lie ahead. God's plan for your life is very real.

My husband Paul and I, having married young, were very close and extremely happy together for 33 years. He was a minister of music and in church-related work for most of those years. Even though I had a career of my own as a high-school teacher, I was always satisfied to be known as "Paul's wife." After he fell ill with a malignant melanoma and died within a few short months, I was overwhelmed. Stunned by the sudden descent of his illness upon us and the devastation of watching him sicken and die, I was further shocked by the reality that I must now make every decision without his support. I felt as alone as I have ever felt in this world.

Getting Through The First Year

People told me that the first year of widowhood would be the most difficult. I don't know how I got through it, except with God's help and some choice Christian friends who provided the human support I needed. I had so many decisions to make. Never having had responsibility for the "business" areas of our marriage, I suddenly found myself confronted by the need to sell a good deal of property and attend to the upkeep of our house and acreage. Selling a truck, a sawmill (Paul's prized possession), a tractor, all the equipment that he had dearly loved to use on our farm — how would I ever know how to do it all, and do it well? With each sale I worried. Was this the price he would have wanted? I felt such a strong need to defend him, now that he was not here to defend himself. I wanted to get the best price — and I wanted it not for me, but for Paul.

Watching Out For The "Vultures"

A remark Paul had once made often came back to me in those difficult days — how people can behave like vultures, swarming around to take advantage of a widow in her distress. More than one man offered me a ridiculous price for some piece of property or equipment, "to help you get rid of things." One of our renters who owed me a lot of money moved out by night, adding insult to injury by hiding the key to the house. Another renter threatened to sue when a tree limb fell on his truck. Every problem seemed monumental — more than monumental — to me.

Overwhelming Feelings

Many times I simply sat down and cried. I was angry at my husband for dying and leaving me in such a predicament. How could I be angry at the poor man? He couldn't help dying. No, he couldn't help it, but neither could I help feeling angry. Human feelings are real, neither good nor bad, just human. We need to acknowledge them as real if we are to work through them so that healing can take place. Yes, sometimes I did feel angry at Paul, even angry at God for allowing me to land in this predicament.

At other times, fortunately, I was able to laugh at myself and my situation. I was not the only widow who had ever had it rough. Going to my Bible for consolation, in the 18th chapter of Luke's Gospel I found Jesus' account of another widow who had a hard time. Centuries pass, but human nature doesn't change. The lesson for me in that little parable was persistence: the widow never gave up seeking fair treatment and a right outcome. All I could do some days was just put one foot in front of the other, taking life one tiny step at a time until I could see my way clear for larger steps.

Most of the time during that first year, I was truly in a daze. The nights seemed endless, and I could not sleep. I was afraid. I was desperately lonely. I kept reliving those last weeks after my husband had become completely paralyzed and thought of how I had prayed for a miracle — a miracle that never happened. Why hadn't God healed him? Why hadn't God taken me? Those were the questions I asked over and over again. Yes, I was sometimes bitter about my fate.

Dealing With Resentments

I know that Christians sometimes can't understand how someone who has lost a spouse may feel bitter. People are quick to tell us that we should never question God. Whether I was questioning God or simply wrestling with my pain, I can't say, but I was certainly bitter. My husband had been a good man, a good witness for the Lord, doing the Lord's work. Yes, I did ask God — Why? Why did he have to suffer? Why did I? Even so, I realized that I wasn't the only one who had such feelings. In our Lord Jesus' crucifixion agony, even He, too, had cried out that great heart-rending "Why?"

While visiting my husband's grave one day, I met another widow, much younger than I. There in the cemetery we spoke about our husbands. Hers had died suddenly, and she was still devastated and very bitter. Freely expressing those feelings to me, she knew I would understand when she said resentfully that every time she looked out her office window she saw "a bunch of S.O.B.s nobody would ever miss if they died." She also told me she was deathly tired of people telling her how much good was going to come from this experience. In the fresh immediacy of our grief, we cannot see how any good can come of any of it.

Yes, we do ask God why, and that is all right. I have never received any answer to my question, but I had to ask it before I could work my way through my sorrow. Whatever God's plan was for Paul's life, and for mine, I had no choice but to accept it by faith and faith alone.

When "Meaning Well" Didn't Help

People mean well. I know that. But most people simply do not know how to console someone who grieves. Often, if they find the courage to say something, anything, it turns out to be the wrong thing. I had to wonder how many times I had been less than comforting to other people before I, too, experienced the pain of losing someone dear.

I had no idea that "just being there" meant so much — usually more than anything that is said or done. I was grateful when a friend would come by and just sit with me for a while, or make an opportunity for us to be together somewhere away from the house. At such times, it was often best if the other person said nothing at all. And I surely welcomed it whenever my friends would allow me to cry. Often a demonstration of true sympathy was the only thing I wanted or needed — the knowledge that someone else also felt the sadness, shared my grief, and shed their own tears in company with me.

The Discomfort Of Others

Most people were uncomfortable when I wanted to talk about my husband. They wanted me to "just get over it" and not dwell on the good things about the past. Yet we need to keep our loved ones alive through memories, for memories are all that we have left. If I had not been able to speak lovingly and gratefully of Paul and his life, I would have been discounting the importance and value of his time upon this earth.

I cannot emphasize enough how extremely important it is for grieving persons to find others who will encourage talk about our loved ones, sharing of pictures, and taking comfort in our sweet memories.

Friends Who Meant The Most

Who helped me most in those trying times? The ones who called to check on me, who invited me out for coffee, or for lunch. How I loved them for it! Those who simply said, "Call me if you need anything" never heard a word from me. I believe my experience in this vein was typical of the experience of anyone who has suffered a loss. A phone call to say, "I've been thinking about you," or "How about meeting me for coffee this morning?" is a gift rarer than words can say.

Practical help is another very welcome gift in such times. If someone had come to mow my lawn, clean my gutters, or see about changing the oil in my automobile, those acts would have been wonderful gifts to me, for suddenly I was burdened with the need to attend to hundreds of details of which I had had no previous experience whatever.

Why Didn't God Take Me?

One reaction I experienced is common to many who are left after a loved one dies — the death wish. I was astonished to discover that I really wanted to die. I thought about taking my own life, and I had enough narcotic medications left over from Paul's last days to accomplish it, keeping them hidden for a very long time. At one point I even foolishly took a mixture of several, hoping it would do me in. Would it have seemed accidental? I didn't know and little cared. Today I am profoundly thankful that my ignorance of drug interactions and medication strengths was enough to save me.

Having previously believed that I was a very strong person emotionally — someone who could handle anything — I was humbled to discover that only a Higher Power would get me through the pain. My faith seemed very weak. I was certainly not the "strong little woman" everyone said I was.

Yet my faith in Christ was the main reason that I could not resort to a focused, intentional means of taking my life, because if I truly believed the Bible and believed what I had been teaching my Sunday-School classes through the years, I had to acknowledge that my loss was God's permissible will for my life, and for Paul. I could not misrepresent my God, knowing that He said that He would always be with me, and that His grace was sufficient. It has been sufficient — more than sufficient. It has been abundant, in every way.

Handling The Holidays

My next challenge during that grim first year was the holiday season. Our Thanksgiving holiday had always been a source of pleasure for me. I always cooked favorite dishes and delicious desserts, for my husband and family loved to eat, and turkey with all the trimmings was always seen as a special treat. The children and grandchildren had always come to our house and stayed all day. Now what was I going to do, and how would I ever get through it? For the first time ever, Thanksgiving seemed to me an occasion when I could give no thanks. The children would have to enjoy their own Thanksgiving and leave me to myself. I really wanted to crawl in a hole and stay there until the holiday was over.

My son Rick, bless him, had other ideas. He called to say that it wouldn't seem right if we all didn't get together, as in all the years of the past. His words reminded me of the way I felt after my own dad died. My mother never had the family together again for a meal. I remember her telling me, "I don't think I will ever laugh again." And at that moment I suddenly lost my own sense of home. My son was right. After listening to what he had to say, I knew that I must have the Thanksgiving meal for our family, rather than focusing so intently on my own distress and leaving everyone else with an even deeper sense of loss than the loss of a father and grandfather.

To make preparations easy, I had a local restaurant cook the turkey and dressing and asked each of the children to bring a dish to share. When we gathered around the table on Thanksgiving day, with a lump in my throat, I took my husband's place. As we said the blessing and looked around at each other, I knew that we still had much to be thankful for in spite of our grief. We had each other. We were still a family, even if diminished by one.

The holidays are always difficult for anyone who mourns, yet there are ways to lighten the load. I know from experience that avoidance is no solution. Some parts of the traditions can be maintained, while adding something new each year.

Christmas is another holiday that can be a time of deep depression and sadness. Many people feel terribly depressed at Christmastime, expecting a joyous holiday while forced to live with a sad reality. This is especially true if a particular family has experienced sad events around Christmastime over the years. One woman I will call Sally never understood why the Christmas season brought such a sense of sorrow to her family, until as an adult she discovered that most of the deaths in the family had occurred around the Christmas season. Today Sally works hard to throw off that cloud of gloom and resist carrying it on to the next generation of her family, who do not understand why it existed at all.

We all have family traditions. We had always had our family get-together on Christmas Eve, but that first year after Paul's death, decorating a tree and rummaging into the boxes of decorations that we had used for so many years just felt like too great a task to undertake. I did not want to put myself through that pain. And so I chose an easier way.

Instead of buying a real tree, as we had done in the past, I purchased an artificial one that was fairly easy to assemble, then bought all new decorations that would appeal especially to the children. I bought a new Nativity scene and other decorations for the house. I bought a beautiful arrangement for Paul's grave and took it to the cemetery before Christmas. When I drove through the gates, I couldn't believe the festive scene. Yes — festivity at the cemetery! Most of the graves had been decorated for the season. Small decorated trees, wreaths, flowers of all kinds, balloons and ribbons. All of this was so new to me — spending time at the cemetery on Christmas Eve — yet I felt compelled to be there, wanting in some way to share our observances with the one member of the family who was no longer with us in the flesh.

Rituals Of Letting Go

Besides just getting through holidays, widows and widowers face other painful tasks, such as disposing of clothing and other personal items. Friends are ready to give plenty of advice, such as, "the quicker the better." Of course, most of these friends haven't lost a spouse. I had to go by my own feelings, and I encourage anyone who is grieving a loss to do the same. Each one of us reacts differently. Some dispose of their loved one's belongings quickly, while others take on this task only when they feel ready.

Some widows or widowers may choose to place good clothing in consignment shops, donate articles to charities, or pass them on to other family members. A grandchild or nephew or niece might like to have something to remember the deceased person by, but hesitates to ask for fear of upsetting the survivor. Many affectionate relatives or friends would love to be given a choice of the deceased one's belongings to cherish in memory.

For me, the process of disposing of personal things was a gradual one, and I needed months to be able to let go. It's all right to keep whatever you want for as long as you want to keep it. After all, you are the one who must feel satisfied. In coping with grief, no one can dictate rules that apply to everyone. The most important thing is to arrive at a solution that feels right, so that you can rest comfortably in the knowledge that you have done a good thing.

Visiting The Grave

Some widows never return to the cemetery, but I found comfort in going. I couldn't shake the feeling that my husband was there. Of course I really knew that he wasn't, but still I wanted to visit and keep fresh flowers on his grave. Irene, an elderly widow, appreciated being able to go to the cemetery and sit on a small bench near her husband's grave. For many months she went there regularly and sat, saying nothing but feeling consoled that he understood and wanted her to be comforted in her grief.

In this regard, too, everyone reacts differently. I visited the cemetery regularly until one day a strange thing happened. As I was driving home after being there, I had an uncanny feeling, as though I could feel my husband's presence with me in the car. I did not feel frightened in the least. God seemed to be telling me that my husband wasn't in that grave, and from that time on I never thought of him as being there again. No longer did I feel that compulsion to visit the cemetery. It was another stage of letting go.

Wedding Rings

Taking off my wedding ring was a difficult task. I was able to do it only when I finally realized that I was no more married with the ring on than I was with it off. Replacing it with another ring seemed the easiest solution for me. Strange how I had never thought about any of these life passages and my responses to them until they happened to me. My engagement ring, too, was something I cherished and wanted to keep, but I didn't want to lead people to believe that I was spoken for, or engaged to be married.

Going Back To Work

Some of the advice people give to grieving persons, fortunately, is good. Many people told me to stay busy, to go places, to be around people at least some of the time. I firmly believe in the strength of this advice after having acted upon it. Just a month after my husband's death, I felt very empty and alone. And when I went back to work, it was with a heavy heart. I was intensely aware that there would be no one to go home to at the end of the day, no one with whom to share the day's happenings.

All the same, I returned to work at the same high school where I had taught for years. My co-workers were sweet and understanding, but I dreaded the prospect of the full school year. And then another strange thing happened, almost like a signal. Reaching far back into my filing cabinet, I touched a rolled-up poster that I hadn't remembered being there. Curiously, I unrolled it to see what it was about.

Now, I love dogs and other animals, and here was a full-length picture of a dog. Oddly enough, I couldn't remember ever seeing this poster before. And even more odd was the fact that this poster of a dog bore a Biblical quotation that spoke directly to my sorrowing spirit:

> *"Eye has not seen, nor ear heard,*
> *Nor have entered into the heart of man*
> *The things which God has prepared*
> *For those who love Him."*

> — *I Corinthians 2:9 (NKJV)*

Call it coincidence or whatever you wish, but I felt that I was being given a message that everything was all right with my loved one and that I, too, should be at peace. Who is to say that God can't use a poster of a dog to call a person's attention to a real truth she may have forgotten? My task and my spirit seemed lighter as I got back to work preparing my room for the incoming students.

Keeping Busy

I'm glad that I stayed busy, glad that I kept on going to church even when I didn't feel like it, glad that I was employed, and glad that I took the time to become involved in recreation such as golf and swimming. Our emotional state is very much interwoven with our physical well-being and our interactions with other people. Even though I still experienced emptiness and loneliness at home, these outside activities helped greatly in my healing process.

Someone has said, "It is impossible to feel sad when taking a brisk walk." It's true. Even the few moments of relief brought about by physical activity can give life a brighter hue.

Social Life Turned Upside Down

It didn't take long for me to realize how different every aspect of my life had become. It seemed suddenly as if the whole world were made for two, not one. Wherever I went, I felt like the fifth wheel. I found myself in a single world, and yet I still felt very much married. No longer did I fit in with married friends — not that they were ungracious, but circumstances were just different. I was no longer interested in swapping recipes, discussing furniture or home decoration, all those things that belonged in a "home," for I didn't feel that I had a home any longer. Having been a wife for so many years, I had come to see keeping house as something I did for someone else.

One dear couple, long-time friends, did continue including me in their activities and even took me with them on a vacation. Single or married, I was still their friend, and that was all that mattered. Now that's true friendship. But they were the exception rather than the rule.

What, Me A Threat?

In addition, I began to see that in the social context I was perceived differently. I was *single!* Married and single men who had previously felt comfortable giving me a friendly hug now kept their distance. Married women whom I had considered friends surprised me by the newly protective stance they adopted towards their husbands in my company. I had never imagined that I could be a threat to anyone's marriage and certainly would never have thought of myself as a woman on the make. I felt hurt by these reactions.

Men and women who have never been widowed (or, for that matter, divorced) don't realize how suddenly your social life simply dries up when you are a person on your own. Movies, trips, sporting events — all the things we had enjoyed in our married life were utterly different now, seemingly inaccessible to us as single persons. We wondered if these would ever be a part of our lives again.

Finally I decided the best thing for me to do was to seek out women in similar circumstances in order to have some social interactions without risking rejection or hurt. Believe me, there were plenty of other widows around. Not long ago I heard former President Jimmy Carter speaking about the disproportionate numbers of widows and widowers in his hometown of Plains, Georgia — at least ten times as many widows as widowers in that small community. Such numbers are typical for most places in America today.

Later I got a good laugh when I heard about a woman in Alabama who brought together a group of widowed friends in order to have someone to enjoy social activities with. These widowed ladies call themselves — The Loose Women!

Growing Stronger

The anniversary of Paul's death was a hard occasion for me, but I got through it without breaking down. I even came to see that I had made some progress in healing from my grief. As my second year of widowhood began, I recognized that things had improved. Many business decisions were behind me, and I was sleeping better and crying less.

By now I was going out frequently with a woman friend (I'll call her Ila) who had lost her husband within a few months of my bereavement. Our friendship was great. We could share experiences, cry, and even laugh at ourselves. At first we made sure that we got back home before dark and never ate in nice restaurants, feeling that we somehow "stood out" as two women without male escorts. We found much pleasure in shopping, for while our husbands were alive, they had never wanted to shop with us. Ila's friendship and companionship was a godsend to me, and I believe my friendship meant much the same to her.

A New Identity

As time passed, I began to consider my own identity and how it had changed. When I had the next batch of checks printed, I changed the way my name appeared. I applied for credit cards in my own name rather than as my husband's wife. I bought a new car — a truly major undertaking. I had never purchased a car by myself, and afterward I went home and cried, because I had no one with whom to share my happiness in the new possession.

The reality of my husband's death continued to sink ever deeper into my life. This was the way it was going to be — nothing could change that. My emotional roller-coaster took me back into the depths of depression again. I knew I had to resist this depression and not let it take over my entire outlook, but every day I had to adjust my attitude all over again.

Widows, Widows Everywhere

During that second year the weekdays went well enough, but the weekends were terribly, terribly lonely. Memories of my companionship with Paul came back very strongly, and I missed him as much as ever. I began noticing how many widows there were in our church — dozens, it seemed to me — and how few widowers. Since statistics show that women outlive men by approximately seven years, I wondered how many other lonely people were having the same feelings that I was having. Was this type of life all there was left for me? A discouraging thought.

Will There Ever Be Another?

At first after Paul's death I was reluctant to say that I would ever marry again. In fact, I would become angry whenever anyone mentioned the possibility. I shunned widowers or divorced men, often being actually rude to them. I didn't want anyone to think that anything — even pure friendship — was going on between me and any man.

It took a few years for me to become comfortable around available men. I realize now how lonely they must have been too, and they really didn't deserve my cold behavior. But in these matters men and women have to become comfortable before they can look at relationships in the light of possibility.

In spite of my fears and resistances, memories of a happy married life and the wonderful relationship that I enjoyed as a wife stirred within me, and I really missed that intimacy and companionship. I knew that if I ever married again, it would not mean that I loved my first husband any less. In fact, it could mean that I had loved him so much that I was willing to take a chance on finding another happy relationship. Well-meaning people give plenty of advice about remarriage. Some approve, some don't. Whatever people say or think, however, life goes on. We must come to our choices as we feel ready and comfortable with them.

Outsides Don't Match The Insides

During those first two years of what I choose to call "Widow Survival," other people paid me compliments: "You have done so well, I admire you so much. You are such an inspiration to me." I thanked them and thanked God that they didn't really know how I felt. By then I had learned to keep quiet about my persistent sorrow. People want to see you survive the traumatic experience of losing your spouse with grace, hoping that they too can survive when their time comes.

The Power Of Being Positive

If you want friends and want to be around other people and be invited places, then after the first few weeks and months are past you must keep your grieving and complaints to yourself. No one wants to be around a sad, crying person — not even your own family. The time comes when everybody decides they have heard enough, and they want you to start living again.

It is not sacrilegious to laugh! Humor helps with the healing process. I used to joke with my friend Ila, telling her that the only black I wore during my mourning days was a black bikini, and that should be enough. We found many things to laugh about even when others may have thought we should keep a long face.

Making It Through

Someone who has never known the loss of a life partner cannot be expected to understand the large and the small issues that must be faced. Until it happened to me, I had no understanding of what such a loss would mean, nor had I given any thought to the plight of the survivor. It never dawned on me how difficult it would be simply to change a light bulb in the ceiling, fix the drip in the faucet, keep the toilet working, or get the lawnmower running. Little things that I had taken for granted — things my husband had done — now became gigantic undertakings for me.

The first time a tire on my car went flat, I was scared to death. I had always called my husband when anything happened to the car, and now he was not there to help. The calamity assumed manageable proportions, however, when I saw that my tire had gone flat directly in front of a service station.

Help Through Others

Now I can see that God was with me during those difficult times. In spite of my pain and heartbreak, many supports were provided. The real-estate agent who took over the sale of our rental property was a great help — a person I could trust completely. A kind neighbor made needed repairs at my house and took care of any plumbing problems. He, too, was truly a godsend. The older widows whom I knew loved me, sympathized, and listened to me. Age is no barrier to sorrow.

When problems arose that I thought I couldn't deal with, God provided for me in many unusual ways. My church family, my pastor, and many friends were a great blessing to me. My three children and their families were very dear and special during the most difficult times. Truly, I was blessed, even at times when my eyes were too filled with tears to see it.

Trusting To God

As my third year of widowhood began, I was determined to live my life for God, whatever lay ahead. I knew that God's purpose for my life was not over yet, and my strongest desire was for God to use me to help dispel other people's darkness, until the day when I would step into the light of His presence myself.

Little did I realize how God was going to accomplish His purpose for me.

Part Two

A Flight

Hold fast to dreams
For if dreams die
Life is a broken-winged bird
That cannot fly.

– Langston Hughes

Many times I have noticed an injured bird and felt sad to know that the bird will soon fall prey to other animals around it. A bird that cannot fly is destined for an early death. A person, too, without a dream for his or her life is spiritually if not physically dead. We must have dreams for our lives if they are to be meaningful and fulfilled.

The next few years would hold a great deal in store for me, for God was working life-changing experiences. I am writing the "rest" of my story (although of course it is not yet complete) in retrospect to show you how God will provide and give meaning to your life as you continue a walk that is sometimes very lonely. You are never really alone — God is there!

Change In The Air

I continued teaching, but I was discontented with my job. It seemed as though I was no longer achieving goals that were important to me as a teacher. Thinking that I probably needed a change of scenery, I requested a transfer to another high school. At first the change seemed exciting. The building was new, and for the first time I would be teaching in an air-conditioned school — something that can make a huge difference in the humid springs and autumns of the South.

I soon discovered what a terrific challenge this school would be for me. Discipline was a problem, along with drug use, disgusting language, and verbal abuse of teachers and other students, as well as a total lack of respect for authority. Not all the students were disruptive, but the bad surely overshadowed the good. Once again I felt dissatisfied in my teaching life. Had God forgotten me? I would have to wait and see.

A New Direction

When that school year ended and summer afforded the respite I needed, a surprising new thought came into my mind. I began to think of going to the seminary to work toward a master's degree in Christian education. I had always had a keen interest in Biblical studies. Was this truly God's leading, or simply my own frustration with teaching? I prayed for guidance. After all, I was 57 years old, anything but the typical seminary applicant.

As school vacation time rolled into its final weeks I still didn't know what to do. I was glad when Frances, one of my fellow teachers, phoned to invite me to have lunch with her and several other teachers. These get-togethers were always fun and uplifting. Perhaps I would feel encouraged to stay in teaching.

After lunch, as the group was breaking up, I invited Frances to come home to visit with me a while longer. As we talked, I felt led to share my concerns about my vocation. I firmly believe that one of the ways God speaks to us most clearly is through other discerning Christians. This teacher friend encouraged me to apply to the seminary and enroll if accepted. I already knew that I had a strong desire for this new direction myself. After my conversation with Frances, I felt even more affirmed that this new undertaking might be God's plan for the next stage of my life.

Uncertain Steps

I first needed to make sure that I had enough money to go to seminary and live without a salary for those two years. In addition, I would need to request a leave of absence from my high-school post. These cautions seemed necessary, because I wasn't quite ready to give up everything I had worked for during many years. I wanted to keep my other options open in case I had been misled about the rightness of the step. Nevertheless, I now had just one month to get ready.

When I applied for a leave of absence, I was told that teachers were not granted leave to attend a seminary. Seeing me on the verge of tears, Mr. J., the kind man who interviewed me, told me that he would see what he could do. Later Mr. J. called back to say I had been granted my year's leave. I was gaining confidence that this move was in God's plan.

An additional requirement was a letter of recommendation from my church. Once that was sent, I had to wait and see whether I would be accepted, knowing that if it happened, I would have to go quickly to find a place to live in a city hundreds of miles away. Only after my acceptance letter came did I inform my children of my decision. I had wanted to be sure the decision was mine alone.

My youngest daughter and her husband, then living in an apartment in my house, agreed to stay on and take care of the whole house for me, as well as any business that might require attention while I was away. Money was provided by the sale of our rental property. In spite of my anxieties, I was beginning to feel more at peace than at any time since my husband's death.

Encouragement From God's Word

My resolve to step out in faith grew. God was preparing the way for me. Recalling these preparations now, I have no doubt that God had used my time of widowhood to further His purposes for my life.

Women who have always led independent lives may think I was foolish to feel afraid to drive on the interstate highway, much less travel alone. But I had never done such things before, and I had to bolster up my courage before I could try. Also, I had never moved out of town by myself, and the prospect was a daunting one. As I began focusing on my weaknesses, a favorite Scripture passage about God's care for us came back to me: *"My grace is sufficient for thee; for my strength is made perfect in weakness" (II Corinthians 12:9).* I was encouraged. God was working!

During the transition that was to come I had still more providential encouragements. For example, the seminary accepted all of my previous graduate hours — a full semester's worth, mostly in psychology — from the university where I had taken courses to renew my teaching certificate. When the registrar told me they didn't usually do that, I concluded he felt sorry for me because of my advanced age and knew that I would need all the help I could get.

A New Home

My next task was to find an apartment. It would have to accept pets, for my little dog Gypsy had been a great comfort to me since my husband's death. Coming home at the end of a day was always less painful when Gypsy was there waiting and happy to see me.

My daughter made the trip with me for moral support and to help me find a suitable place to live. With only a half day for the task, we began our search. Early in the morning I found an apartment near the seminary that I really liked, but the manager told us she had just rented it. Seeing how disappointed I was, she told me to call back later in the day in case the new tenant failed to qualify. Now, in all charity, I couldn't pray for the man's credit to be lacking, but a part of me was still hoping that he would not get that apartment.

We kept looking. I was discouraged after looking at many apartments and finding none that seemed right. My daughter, bless her, insisted that we call the manager of the first apartment complex. We called, and when there was no answer, my daughter promptly declared that we would drive back there on the chance of finding the manager in. How thankful I was for her encouragement and perseverance. I might have given up otherwise.

When we arrived back at the office, the manager met us with a big smile. "I'm so glad you came back! The man's credit didn't go through. The apartment is yours!" Once again, I had to believe that that particular apartment was a part of God's plan for me, and that He was working things out for my good.

And so, with the support of friends and family, I left the city where I had lived for decades to begin my new adventure. Strangely, I had no fears. I was actually excited. I suspected that some of my friends thought I was making a foolish mistake, but if there were doubters, I was thankful that they kept quiet about it. Others were very encouraging to me. I was beginning to get some inkling of the new purpose in living that beckoned in the months ahead. I could see that it was possible for me to find new meaning in life, new happiness, new satisfactions.

A Godsent New Friend

Although I did not yet know it, a special friend was waiting for me in that apartment complex who would make the transition far more pleasant for me. As I was unpacking and arranging my furniture in the new place, a knock came at the door, and when I answered, a very attractive woman stood in the doorway.

"Hi, Jane. I'm Barbara," she said. The apartment manager had told her that I was a new seminary student, and since she was a new student too, she had dropped by to meet me. To my surprise, I learned that she, too, was a widow, with two small children about the same age as my grandchildren. Barbara and her children were renting a unit just across the street from mine.

Having this young lady enter my life was no coincidence. She would be a great source of strength and support for me in the months to come, and I would be able to be of help and support to her as well. Yes, God was working.

Insecurities Set In

My first experiences at the seminary were a far cry from what I had expected. I had been a teacher for over twenty years — a professional person. Now I became a student, in a totally different league. These "kids" — the other seminary students — were extremely intelligent and well informed. Most of the professors were much younger than I. I was beginning to feel very insecure, especially after hearing that I would be required, along with all the other new students, to take a series of tests. Oh, dear. I was usually the one who gave the tests.

Disappointment With A Purpose

I got through all the tests except the English test. I knew that unless I made a certain score, I would be required to take an extra, remedial class for no credit, although it would count on my grade-point average. No problem for me, an English teacher, right?

In taking the test I carefully applied each rule of grammar, knowing that I was correct. The crucial thing I forgot was that the test was *timed*. Being so extra-cautious, I didn't finish in time, and all the unanswered questions were counted as incorrect. I failed by three points. Talk about humiliation!

Can you imagine that this let-down turned out to be a blessing for me? Yes, it did. Time would pass before I could see it as a preparation for something yet to come. Remember, God knows our future. *"All things work together for good to them that love the Lord,"* the Scripture tells us. Yes, they do, even when it is not at all clear to us at the time.

Discouragement And Determination

As a widow beginning a strange new life, I often reflected upon a poem by Louisa Fletcher that spoke strongly to me. In it, she spoke of a "wonderful place called the Land of Beginning

Again" where mistakes and heartaches and grief "could be dropped like a shabby old coat at the door and never be put on again." Many days as I struggled to make a place for myself at the seminary, I hoped mightily that I would find myself in that Land of Beginning Again, close by a rubbish-heap where I could drop my heartaches and my grief.

When days seem long and loneliness sets in like a drab grey curtain, we just naturally wish for a change. Although we may wish to simply close the door on yesterday and live just for today, that's not always easy for those of us who are widowed. Our past seems much happier to us than our present state or our future.

Nevertheless, I was determined to make my days at the seminary count. I had much to learn and many challenges. I knew it wouldn't be easy, but I was determined to give it my best efforts. My classes were extremely interesting, and I was eager to learn, although I soon realized that this wasn't an ordinary Bible study course or Sunday-School class. Being a professional person and finding these courses so difficult, I knew I was not the first who had ever felt that way.

After getting back the grades on my first tests, I truly began wondering what I was doing there. Had I made a mistake in setting out upon this new direction for my life? Finally I concluded that my presence must be intended to make all the other students feel good about themselves.

As an older student, I had many concerns. Being human, after all, I didn't want to look stupid. One precaution I took was to use great care in merely walking about the campus, because I didn't want to embarrass myself by falling. When a young person falls, not much is thought about it, but when you're older and you trip and fall, everyone wants to rush to call the paramedics.

I had also learned that I would have to study twice as hard as the younger students in order to absorb all the challenging new material. Tests made me particularly nervous. Much of the time, I felt uneasy and anxious. And yet I kept on keeping on.

Others Who Cared

As I became more comfortable in my classes, I recognized how thoughtful and friendly the younger students really were. When we got together to review and study for tests, suddenly everyone seemed to be the same age. We became like a family. The male students told me to call them if I ever had car trouble, an offer that I certainly appreciated. If I had been studying with Barbara, my friend across the street, she always watched to be sure I got safely back to my apartment afterward. She typed my papers, and I provided babysitting for her two children when she needed help. We joined the same church and enjoyed social things together when there was time.

Dreams And Inspiration

Of course, not every grieving widow or widower has a burning desire to return to school, change careers, or even take up a career at all. That's fine. We're all different, but I believe everyone benefits by pursuing a dream of some sort. Any demanding task is a worthwhile one.

I like to read about people who have overcome unfortunate or unsatisfactory circumstances, for in almost every case, a positive attitude was the element that enabled them to achieve success. Listening to sermons about maintaining a positive attitude appealed to me. One evening I stood in line for two hours to have a book signed by a popular TV pastor. Two of his admonitions — "Turn your scars into stars" and "If it's going to be, it's up to me" — helped me through some very discouraging times. These words, along with the inspiration I found in the Bible, helped me to believe in myself, to believe that I could rise to this challenge and succeed.

Living Into God's Will

Although I am not foolish enough to imagine that I can be anything I want to be, I most certainly do believe that I can be anything God wants me to be. In enrolling in the seminary, I believed I was doing what God wanted me to do, working toward a particular goal.

God may have something entirely unexpected for you to do with your life. Ila, the widowed friend with whom I had spent a great deal of time before I entered the seminary, was given a very special task. Her two young grandchildren came to live with her, and God gave her the responsibility of helping them to grow into two fine adults. To me, her task seemed much larger and more demanding than my move out of town to enter school.

God certainly filled the void in her life, while giving her the strength and knowledge to rear those children. I really believe God leaves us here on this earth until our work is finished. This Scripture verse *(Psalm 138:8, NIV)* says it well:

> *"The Lord will fulfill His purpose for me;*
> *Your love, O Lord, endures forever.*
> *Do not abandon the works of your hands."*

A Little Headway

As my first semester ended, I was well pleased by the improvement in my grades. Now I could see that I was indeed going to win that master's degree.

I soon had to make a choice, however. My leave of absence had been granted for just one school year. The question now arose: do I give up teaching — job security, full retirement benefits, and all the rest — in order to finish the course?

I still lacked one semester of earning my degree. Would I have to withdraw from seminary and postpone the remainder of my graduate work? What money I had would not last forever — of that I was sure. On the other hand, I knew that if I didn't stay in school, I probably would never go back. It was Decision Time.

A Faith Decision

When I phoned the school system's central office, personnel had changed, and I had to deal with people I did not know. Mr. S., now the man in charge, didn't understand why I had qualified for a leave in the first place and made it clear that I had no choice at that point except to resign my teaching position. I said I would write a letter to that effect.

As I hung up the phone, my emotions were a mixture of anxiety and the certainty that I should move ahead. I had no job security, yet I had every confidence that I was doing what I was supposed to do. How did I know? Only through a sureness in my heart, grounded in prayer. I was being led step by step, without being able to see to the end of the road.

The following Sunday when I went to church, the choir sang "Great Is Thy Faithfulness." God always reassures us when we act upon our trust in Him. Knowing my troubled state of mind, Barbara, sitting next to me, leaned over to whisper, "I believe that song is for you." Every time I have heard that song since, I remember that special moment of encouragement. Yes, God is faithful, and He calls us to be faithful, too.

Older Friends

In the apartment complex where I lived, I had several older neighbors and friends, one in particular I'll call Helen. Helen often brought over some of her good home cooking to share with me, and we enjoyed talking about our life experiences together. She was in her 70s and still working as a babysitter. Many cold mornings I would see Helen outside starting her old car, scraping frost from her windshield, or lifting the hood to pour in more oil. This woman was a survivor, someone who had dealt with many life problems and was still out there doing her best. I knew I had no right to grumble about my lot.

God has blessed me with the friendship of many wonderful older people who have ministered to me in countless ways. We never know how God is going to use us to influence or guide others. For some, the assignment is to express hospitality, help out in the church nursery, sing in the choir, or visit the shut-ins. Whatever the task God has for us, however humble or mundane, I believe that He wants us to accept it with a grateful heart and true dedication.

Breaking Into Print

Feeling prompted to write an article about the influence of my special older friends, I submitted it to a denominational periodical and achieved my first appearance in print. I've always loved and admired many elderly persons, but at that point I had no idea that a few years later I would hold a paid position in a church, working with senior adults. I had thought that perhaps I might be working with singles, which was becoming an important part of church memberships, but fortunately for me, God still had a lot of training ahead for me.

While I was in graduate school I often felt God's nearness to me. During one term, for instance, I enrolled in a class entitled "Phenomenology and Existentialism." The whole first week passed before I even learned how to pronounce the course title. I had no background in philosophy, but I needed this course. It was a small class that became even smaller as several dropped out. I was very ill at ease, because I didn't understand the textbook, and we were to have a test every week. I asked God to show me how to manage to pass this one.

The class included just one other woman, Lisa, and before the first test, Lisa asked if we could get together to study. Wonder of wonders, I discovered that she had been a philosophy major. Deeply thankful to God for supplying my need, I made a good grade on the test and eventually on the course. Yes, God supplies our needs *if we but ask.* Today I readily admit that although I could repeat for the professor what the professor had laid out for us, I still don't understand phenomenology and existentialism.

Follow Your Leadings

If I were to give advice to any widow or widower, it would be this: "As fearlessly as possible, move ahead with whatever you are inclined to do. If you are afraid, find sources of affirmation and press on all the same." For some, training in new job skills may be required. Others may wish to return to a profession practiced in younger years. Those fortunate to be in good health have no reason not to follow their inclinations, and anyone whose health won't permit an unlimited choice can still find something worthwhile to occupy his or her energies.

We are never too old to follow our dreams, or to claim a new dream.

The accomplishments of older people always amaze and inspire me. When I came across a column by The Rev. Gordon Greenwell in a church bulletin, I cut it out and saved it for the encouragement it contained. Pastor Greenwell wrote:

Between the ages of 70 and 83, Commodore Vanderbilt earned more than $100 million.

Alfred Lord Tennyson was 83 when he wrote his great poem "Crossing the Bar."

John Wesley at 83 wrote for 15 hours a day.

At 86 Charles Wesley was still preaching two sermons each day.

Cato learned Greek after he was 80 years old.

Daniel Webster was 70 when he wrote his great dictionary.

The entrepreneur J. C. Penney worked strenuously up until the age of 95.

Mary "Grandma" Moses didn't even start painting until she was 79.

Being aware of these senior citizens' accomplishments made me feel quite young when I began my second career at age 61. The Scriptures declare, *"Fear not, for I am with thee. For I am thy God. I will strengthen thee; yea, I will uphold thee with the right hand of my righteousness" (Isaiah 41:10, KJV).* I know that this is a true word, for I have lived it myself.

Importance Of Community

When any one of us is left without a life partner, our first task must be to resist becoming isolated. God created us to be inter-dependent — to be a community of mutually supportive women and men friends. "No man is an island," the poet John Donne so aptly put it. We need to reach out to other people. We need to keep as active and involved as possible. We were born for community and interdependence.

One of my dear friends, whom I shall call Martha, was widowed after also losing her only child to an incurable disease. At the time of her severest grief, Martha mostly just sat in a chair and slept. She didn't go anywhere or do anything. I felt so sad for her, and I feared that she would soon die if she stayed glued to that chair and that house. When I suggested to Martha that she try going back to work, her answer was always the same: "No, I can't do it. What if I went back and I couldn't do it?"

Finally through the help of other friends, she was persuaded to try. Not only could she do the work, she did it extremely well. Martha has received awards for being "Salesperson of the Week," "Most Courteous Employee," and the like, and is still working at age 75. Even though she has no family left, she has a multitude of admiring friends and acquaintances. She is not completely alone, and her life has purpose and value.

Benefits Of Reaching Out

Once we are left alone, whatever activities and involvements we may choose, although we may undertake them with the intent of helping someone else, the greatest benefit and help will ultimately be to ourselves. Time is our great healer, and even though we never stop loving the ones who have died and left us, life does get easier to bear. Whatever we choose to do, above all, we must go on living a useful life. Believe me, when we do that, life does get better.

A Bright Spot

While I was at seminary, one of my friends, knowing that I was having a pretty tough struggle to make it through, gave me a wonderful gift — tickets to the Kentucky Derby. Having watched this annual event on television in the past, I had never imagined being there in person to see those thrilling horses make the "Run for the Roses." Yet there I was. Sometimes when we have pushed ourselves to consume a nutritious if not sensational meal, God gives us dessert.

One Challenge Ends, Another Begins

The remaining year and a half of graduate school passed quickly for me. Before I realized how fast the months had flown, it was time for graduation. My children and two of my best friends from home joined me for this important occasion. I had purchased a small pinky-finger graduation ring, which I still wear with pride, and I bought a white leather coat, pretending it was a graduation gift from my husband.

When I had seen him receive the same degree 30 years before, I had completed only two years of college. Later, after three children and 15 years, I had completed my undergraduate degree. Now that I had earned the graduate degree as well, I knew he would be extremely proud of me. Even though I was the oldest member of my graduating class, it made no difference to me — I knew I had earned that master's degree in Christian education.

As we prepared to leave, my children loaded up the rental truck with my belongings. Seminary days were behind me. Goodbyes were over. What next?

It surely would not be what I had expected. Someone has observed, accurately, that life is what happens to you while you're making other plans.

Part Three

A Dark Night

As I think about the next three years of my widowhood, I associate those times with a period of darkness. When it is dark, we don't see clearly. We may stumble and fall because we can't see obstacles in our path. We have no clear understanding of what is going on. Storms seem worse at night, when it is dark. I was frightened by shadows of doubt and financial difficulties. I couldn't help wondering if I would ever see the proverbial light at the end of my tunnel of anxiety.

I prepared a new résumé for prospective employers in church-related work, and the seminary also sent out résumés for graduates whenever inquiries came in. Right away, I began to have doubts about my future employment as I considered the "probablys." Probably I was too old. Probably a woman would have less chance of being hired than a man. I thought that I was just being realistic. Had I forgotten about faith?

Searching the Scriptures for encouragement, I found it in Hebrews, Chapter 11. The first verse of that chapter on faith contains the words that spoke most clearly to me: *"Now faith is being sure of what we hope for and certain of what we do not see" (NIV)*. It's easy to say we have faith, but yet we still really want to *see*. That is only human.

I couldn't know that God was getting ready to teach me many things. I was soon to discover that living by faith can be quite exciting. Today, looking back, I wouldn't take anything for the experiences God permitted me in the three years that followed.

Waiting For The Unknown

After my December graduation, January back at home was a dreary month. Accustomed to being surrounded by lively young people at the seminary, I found the silence and inactivity of my now-solitary existence most oppressive. My friends were all working or otherwise involved, and I was fast becoming bored and depressed.

The empty days were so long, with nothing to look forward to but even emptier evenings and nights. Self-pity was taking over, robbing me of my optimistic outlook on the world.

Casting about for solutions, I decided to begin attending a different church from the one I had gone to in the past, because the new one had a large singles department, even older singles. In drawing me to this new faith community, I know now that God was helping me to heal, to find new ways of living, to discover new meaning in my unattached life.

I didn't know anybody in the adult singles class at first, but everyone there was very friendly and seemed to welcome my company. This group would become a great blessing to me. Many in the group were widowed; some were divorced. There were men and women of various ages. I was with people *just like me* who had much in common. Even though the church was quite a large one, this singles group formed a family-like unit of encouragement around each of its members.

Doing What I Found To Do

One winter morning, with no schedule to keep and no place in particular to go, as I was taking my time reading the paper and drinking my coffee, I noticed an ad for volunteers. Still with no prospect of a job, I concluded that volunteer work might be a useful solution to my inactivity. And so I signed up as a volunteer with a national charity.

Immediately I found myself swamped with work. Envelopes had to be stamped, kits stuffed, endless phone calls made, and volunteers were needed to work at local malls providing free screenings. This experience was tremendously good for me. It got me out of the house and took my mind off myself, but even more important was the fact that I met new people. In the course of the screenings, I also found out about a health isssue of my own, which I promptly took steps to remedy.

One of my fellow volunteers, Louise, had recently moved with her husband from the North and knew very few people in the area. I soon discovered that Louise was truly in need of a friend, for she had a heart-breaking problem and needed someone to listen and comfort her. Her adult child had recently committed suicide, and neither she nor her husband had been aware of any problem, as this child was married and lived away from home. I was glad she confided in me, for I knew from experience that talking about a concern can release some of the pent-up emotions that drag us down physically and mentally. I was humbly grateful when Louise told me she believed God had sent me there, because she really needed someone with whom she could discuss her deep hurt. An opportunity to serve, and to minister.

Still without employment, I went on to volunteer as a tutor in an adult literacy program. I was happy to think how different this experience would be from teaching apathetic or hostile high-school students, for these people would be motivated and truly eager to learn. When I met Ruby, the 62-year-old woman assigned to me, I sensed immediately that God had brought us together. We were of approximately the same age, which provided an effortless bond. During our introductory conversation, when I asked Ruby why she wanted to improve her reading ability, her answer came promptly: "I would just love to be a Sunday-School teacher. I want to be able to read the Bible better and be of service in my church." I understood that motivation and could support it wholeheartedly.

Those tutoring sessions came to mean the world to me. After working hard all day in the university's housekeeping department, Ruby came ready and eager to learn. After our regular lesson I always selected a passage of Scripture for her to read aloud to me, and after reading it, she would always ask, "Now, what does it mean?" That was one time that the book of Revelation wasn't on the reading list! Again, God was using me in ways where I had never gone before.

If you are lonely, seemingly without meaningful occupation, the best advice I can give you is to volunteer at least part of your time. It is a tremendously rewarding experience. For someone who has been left alone, breaking away from your house, your worries, your self-absorption is absolutely vital. Doing something beneficial for someone else will be even more beneficial for you. The first steps may not be easy, but it is well worth making the effort to find your niche.

Financial Worries Answered

My financial situation was becoming critical. The expenses of owning a home and other property were constantly draining my bank account. I really needed income, yet I still had no paying job. I concluded that I needed two different résumés — one for religious work and another for secular employment. I followed up on many ads in the newspaper and went to many interviews, most of which left me feeling depressed. It was demoralizing going for job interviews at age 59. Didn't God realize that I was running out of money?

As my graduate degree was in religious studies, I had not thought about employment in a secular educational institution. Nevertheless, one day my son telephoned me to say that he knew a community-college faculty member who needed a teacher for a remedial English course. Excitement took hold as I called and was given an appointment for an interview. I was thankful to learn that my master's degree qualified me for this position.

Another new blessing — I was hired. Although it was only for one semester, this employment qualified me for the same position in subsequent semesters, with the number of classes depending upon the number of students who had flunked the qualifying exam. When I was called on to teach three separate sections of the course I was elated, because the amount of my paycheck was based on the number of classes I taught. God was taking care of me. How could I have doubted Him?

My students, ages 18-30, were very receptive and, like Ruby, eager to gain the necessary skills. Some were returning to school after having a family or pursuing another career. Some were recent high-school graduates. Some were embarrassed because they were deficient and had to take the course, while others felt they were too old to have to begin at an elementary level.

With all their issues I could identify strongly. My own past experiences gave me an understanding of their fears and disappointments. I remembered how low I had felt when I had been required to take remedial English at the seminary. When they learned about that, they relaxed, knowing that I was not an adversary but a kindred spirit. They were eager to have my advice and followed it when given.

At semester's end I was in a better financial position, but the improvement couldn't last long unless something else turned up. At this point I decided to sell my piano. It was only taking up space, and it was as good as new. When the piano sold for a very good price, I could breathe easy for another month at least.

Pride And Pretense

During the summer that followed, I had plenty to do just keeping up with the mowing of the acre lot my house occupied. Sometimes when the riding mower was broken, I used the push mower, pretending I was doing it for my health. Certainly the exercise was good for me.

I made excuses to friends at church when they would invite me to go out to eat after the services. I didn't want to tell them I didn't have the money — not even for a hamburger. I didn't want anyone feeling sorry for me, or even knowing my circumstances. God was supplying my needs, and the extras I could do without.

From time to time I received inquiries from various churches, along with questionnaires to fill out and return, but not one produced a job offer. When nine months had passed since my graduation and still no vocational opportunities had turned up, I began to feel deep uncertainty for the first time about my income. For someone alone, this can be a very frightening predicament. I relied on prayer and God's Word for encouragement, knowing that I must do whatever I could and then turn the rest over to Him. He gives us grace on a daily basis, and I had to trust in Him day by day — at times just hour by hour, or minute by minute.

Learning To Receive

Once again I secured employment at the community college for the fall. Whew! Many times money came from unexpected sources. My church gave me scholarship money several times. Friends sometimes included money in a card, signing it, "From one who's been there." After being a self-reliant person for most of my life, I was now learning how blessed it can be to receive. I would have preferred to be on the giving end instead of in need, yet these generous expressions of support truly warmed my heart.

God was providing for me through so many people and circumstances that, believe it or not, I was generally happy during those days — a little anxious now and then, but nevertheless happy. In the fearful days immediately following Paul's death, I had wondered whether I could ever be happy again, and now it was a reality. I was healthy, thank the Lord. I had many friends. I had a caring Heavenly Father. I just accepted it all one day at a time and was thankful.

The Joys Of Laughter

These were not all serious days by any means. One evening Ila, my widow friend with whom I often went out for a meal or a movie, had invited me to join her for dinner at a restaurant. As I stopped by to pick her up, her adult son asked where we were going, and when Ila mentioned a particular riverside restaurant, he was shocked. "Mom! You and Jane shouldn't be going there! That's where women go to get picked up by men!"

"Why do you think we're going?" was Ila's prompt, spunky reply. I loved it. There was still fun in our lives, and we were determined to hang on to it. What a wonderful turn-around — our children were worrying about us, instead of the other way around.

Of course Ila and I never went bar-hopping, but we did sometimes use the term just for fun between ourselves. We had both reached the point of letting people think whatever they wanted to about our social lives. I used to say jokingly I wished I were having as much fun as my neighbors thought I was.

I still had not dated anyone. Oh, I wasn't against dating; I just hadn't met anyone who interested me in that way. My late husband was a tough act to follow, and I couldn't help judging other men against that standard. Although I was at least beginning to imagine the possibility of finding another happy partnership — a healthy change for me — I also wondered if there would ever be another man in my future.

One attribute I have always been able to claim is being realistic. I knew that most of the men my age wanted younger women, and available men my age or older were very few and far between. One day I heard a senior-citizen TV comedienne joke, "You know, it's very discouraging trying to find a man. Most of the ones my age are like parking spaces — either taken or handicapped." That really gave me a good laugh. Yet I was thankful that I had passed the stage of being afraid to enjoy a man's company, which gave me cause for hope.

Longing For Intimacy

Yes, I thought about sex. Just because a person is a Christian doesn't mean that healthy sexual drives are dead, or that she or he is less of a woman or less of a man. When I was happily married, I enjoyed sex with my husband. God had created these desires in me, and it was only normal that I would miss this intimate relationship when I no longer had it. How I envied my friends who still had their husbands and were happy in their marriages.

I did discover, to my disappointment, that some men — even married men or men in long-term relationships — interpreted my single status to mean that I was available for sex. Sometimes friendliness can be mistaken for flirtation, and perhaps that was my difficulty. I have always been a lively, enthusiastic person, someone who enjoys people, and some of my approaches to men may have been misperceived. If I had been married, however, the situation would have been totally different. Widowhood can get complicated!

A Job Had To Be Found

As more time went by and no full-time employment turned up, I had to swallow my pride and apply to become a substitute teacher — a thankless job, in my view. The pupils treat you like a babysitter and often with far less respect than they accord the regular teacher. You are called in at the last minute, and frequently the regular teacher has left no instructions. Even so, I was warmly received by my fellow teachers and their principals in the local high schools.

At the same time, I applied for a full-time teaching position, but I couldn't get one. Someone younger without experience could be hired more cheaply and wouldn't collect as much pension as I would qualify for. My track record was good; nevertheless, I remained unemployed. No churches had responded positively to my résumés. Had I been wrong again in thinking that God had something in His plan for my life?

When autumn came, I was teaching just one morning class at the community college — not enough to support me. With some misgivings, I took an afternoon job at a church day-care center. Now God really presented me with a challenge. I was put in charge of a group of ten little 3-year-olds. It had been a long time since I had had much dealings with children of that young age. I only lasted in the job for about four weeks, and I began every morning of those four weeks praying for the strength just to make it through. By day's end I was always exhausted, and I stayed exhausted until I turned in my resignation.

To my dismay, the young woman in charge of the day-care center told me that she, too, was a graduate of the seminary, and that it had taken her three years to find even that job. I had been out of school for two, and it looked as though I might tie her record or surpass it. I could only pray that would not be the case.

Reviewing my resources, I decided to sell off a strip of land, which helped me financially for a while. I became a paid tutor, which actually brought in good money for any hour's work. But when I went to the bank to see about refinancing my house and property, the bank officer, who had known my husband and spoke fondly of him, told me the bank had to turn me down. I burst into tears. Even as I write this story years later, I get emotional recalling that day. Whatever could I do?

A Solution Out Of The Blue

I remembered old movies in which a widow couldn't make the payments on her house, and the mortgage-holder came and took the house from her. Could the same thing happen to me? In my desperation, I told my trusted real-estate agent friend about my predicament — the same agent who had sold some property for me before. Now he offered, on behalf of his company, to refinance my loan. The payments wouldn't begin for several months, when I should be better off financially. God had come through for me again. Another burden lifted! How thankful I was for this Christian friend whose decisions were taken with people in mind, instead of money.

I was counting my last $50 when this understanding was reached, the week before Thanksgiving. Feeling profoundly blessed, I went to a local charity and donated $25 to provide a Thanksgiving meal for someone who would have none. It felt great! As I was leaving the place it occurred to me that anyone who saw me would probably think I was there to receive a Thanksgiving meal, instead of to donate one.

More Surprising Opportunities

As time went on, I fretted that I still had only part-time employment, not realizing how very valuable these working experiences would prove to be. After quitting the day-care job, I interviewed with a community action group, but in the midst of the interview it dawned on me that I was applying for a position for which I was not qualified. I told the interviewer that I believed I had made a mistake. To my amazement, she hired me for another position that I did not even know was available.

The action group offered free services to unemployed persons and others who needed to upgrade their skills. I would teach communications skills to women who had lost their factory jobs and were now trying to fit themselves for other occupations. The participants had been out of school for many years, yet the diversity of this class made it an extremely interesting and rewarding one.

One of my younger pupils was on welfare. As kindly as I could, I asked her why she had not found a job, and she told me that however much she would like to be off welfare, it entitled her to free childcare and a better income than she could make out working and paying for childcare. I was fast discovering how the system worked, or didn't work, for the long-term betterment of its clients.

Soon after starting at the action group I saw that another part-time job would be good for me, because I had the time available and could use the extra income. How full of surprises life is! My daughter told me that a friend of hers needed someone to market and coordinate riverboat luncheon cruises for senior citizens. It was certainly not the job I might have imagined the Lord providing for me, but with my desire for novelty and fun in life, I jumped at it. Cindy, the young woman who hired me, became a very dear friend. We worked together well, and I discovered that I loved the job.

Sharing an office with others who worked on the boat, I looked forward to going to work in the mornings, and being on the river was a special pleasure. I had always loved the water. Now my job also required me to call on various senior adult groups, church and civic organizations, nursing homes, and assisted-living facilities, many of them looking for social activities. The boat company provided two free dinner cruises, so getting the leaders interested was easy.

In addition to the office work, I had responsibilities on board the boat during the actual cruises, arriving early to help the college-student waiters and waitresses. We had to be sure that before we pulled away from the dock, all the food, which had been prepared outside, was on board, along with anything else that we might need during the cruise.

These buffet luncheons included generous amounts of food, with music to provide a relaxing mood. After the meal we played Bingo, and I handed out prizes from the gift shop. When I chose "volunteers" for a horse-race game, these older folks had great fun seeing their peers crazily riding a stick-horse. We ended the cruise with a sing-along, including plenty of old favorites.

Then my responsibilities expanded. With the luncheon cruises well established, I began working dinner cruises that included gospel music by quartets, soloists, duets, and the like. I made many new friends and rediscovered some former acquaintances. My job was simply to see that everyone was well served and comfortable.

Later on I was asked to help with the Christmas cruises, for which the boat was beautifully decorated. My daughter and son-in-law provided the musical entertainment for these events, and I enjoyed hearing them, a privilege I rarely had.

This part-time job had come to provide a great part of my social life. Seeing other people have fun gave me pleasure and reminded me that I could have fun, too. After the cruises, the captain and all the employees sat down to enjoy a free meal, with delicious food. This job really had its perks.

Not Home Free Yet

For the first couple of years after seminary I was able to continue my student-rate medical insurance. But now that coverage was running out. At my age, any individual medical insurance would be expensive, and part-time work never carries such benefits. As I had done in the past whenever I had a hurdle to get over, I asked God to help me when the time came.

Soon a department head at a different community college from the one where I had been teaching asked if I would teach one class during the summer. As my work at the action group was drawing to an end, this seemed an opportune time to take on something new, and I was happy to hear that I would make more money.

Fortunately, I am an early riser, for the class met at 8:00 A.M. 30 miles from my home. I drove to the college early, taught the class, returned home and graded papers, caught a quick nap, and went on to the riverboat, finishing up my day around 10:30 P.M. Not bad for a senior citizen!

The only drawback was returning home so late at night. I imagined that "everybody" knew I was alone, and my house sat far back from the main road, with no near neighbors. Sometimes you have to do what you have to do. I just used common sense where my personal safety was concerned and prayed that God would give me peace about these fears. A familiar Scripture passage helped me during this time:

> *"The Lord will keep you from all harm —*
> *he will watch over your life;*
> *the Lord will watch over your coming and going*
> *both now and forever more."*

> — *Psalm 121:7-8, NIV*

After a few nights of this schedule had passed, I no longer felt nervous or afraid. God had given me the peace that I had prayed for.

But I still had another fear to conquer — our town's interstate-highway accesses, which seemed very dangerous to me. With traffic at its worst in the mornings when I left for work, the only thing to do was get onto the interstate as quickly as possible and hope for the best. Keeping my driving skills up to par was essential, for otherwise I would become isolated with no means of making a living, trapped by my fears.

Whenever rainy weather added to the hazard, I was a nervous wreck. I began every day with a Bible reading before starting for work, and on one particular morning as I was reading, I heard rain pouring down and thunder and lightning as well. I started praying, acknowledging my fear and asking God to help me, when one special verse just seemed to jump off the page:

> *"When you pass through the waters,*
> *I will be with you."*

> — *Isaiah 43:2, NIV*

Now, that verse was taken out of context, but in my moment of need, it gave me a very real sense of God's presence and loving care. Many times we just need reassurance, and He finds ways to reassure us when we ask. In the same deeply loving way, Jesus reassured his disciples many times when they were afraid.

A Church Calls

Then another unexpected phone call came. The caller was the pastor of the church I had attended before I entered the seminary, which I had always considered my home church. He asked whether I might be interested in an interim position as educational director. Of course I was interested — even though it would be another part-time position. The pastor told me he would soon be meeting with the personnel committee to work out the details. I was delighted.

When I went in for the interview, I found myself surrounded by friendly people whom I had known for many years. My husband had served as minister of music and education in this very church when we were just a young couple with three small children. Now the pastor was recommending that they pay me half of what they had been paying a full-time director and, in addition *pay my medical insurance.* God was meeting all my needs.

From my first day on the job, although I loved the work and the people, I knew I had a great deal to learn. Education is one thing, but experience is truly the great teacher. This church was giving me my first opportunity in a church-related vocation — the vocation I had prepared for in attending the seminary. My job was demanding, for I was expected to juggle responsibilities in at least five different areas. I went at it with a good will, however, and soon was extremely busy but contented, teaching a college class, working on the riverboat, and assuming these new responsibilities at the church. In spite of an extremely full schedule, my burdens seemed light.

As I gave my best efforts to every area of activity specified, I felt affirmed that God's plan for my future was opening up in a new phase, for the majority of members in this church were senior adults — the group where I would ultimately find my own niche and most rewarding field of ministry.

When our senior pastor accepted a call to a church in another town, he left behind a church staff that included a full-time music and senior-adult minister, a part-time youth director, two secretaries, a custodian — and me. As the personnel committee began the search for an interim pastor to serve until a permanent pastor was hired, I suspected I was about to get more experience than I had bargained for.

Working on the boat I had become accustomed to using a microphone — a skill that proved helpful when I had to bring the children's sermon on Sunday mornings. As the little ones gathered around me to hear my brief talk, I noticed that all the adults were listening as well. The children were precious, but I never knew what their responses would be. Children are completely honest, and usually uninhibited!

The First Date

Just before Christmas I was surprised to have a phone call from a man I had known during my high-school and college years. Charles lived about 100 miles away, and his wife had recently died. In the way that women know these things, I recalled that far back in our past, Charles had been interested in me. Although I wanted to see him and talk over old times, I knew that at some point I would have to tell him that there would never be anything between us but friendship.

With the holidays approaching, knowing how lonesome that time could be for someone newly widowed, I invited him to come and go with me on one of the riverboat Christmas cruises. He accepted readily. As the day drew closer, I began to feel anxious, for although I was flattered that someone wanted to be with me — someone who knew my past and had also known Paul — this would be my first date since being widowed.

The evening began pleasantly as we talked over old times and mutual acquaintances, although I sensed from the beginning that this old friend had something more than friendship in mind. Knowing that I could never be intimately involved with Charles, I finally spoke my feelings honestly and as kindly as I could. He seemed to accept what I said and asked when we parted if we could be "buddies." I said that would be fine. So after that Charles would occasionally call me or write letters that began, "Dear Buddy." When I learned a few years later that he had died suddenly from a heart attack, I was glad that I had been kind but honest with him. Life is so short!

As time went by, I was finding myself more at ease around eligible men. Some of my readers may wonder, "But where did you find them?" I met men at church, at the community college, and through friends and my cruise connections. Yet in spite of several opportunities I still saw no one whom I cared to date. I preferred just being a friend, with no expectations. I believed that unless I really desired to spend time in a particular man's company, it would be wrong to accept his invitation merely for the sake of a nice meal.

Of course, some women are very comfortable accepting an invitation purely for the pleasure of going out. That's fine, if you are comfortable with it. All of us are different — and those who do accept invitations without hesitation always have the possibility of meeting a friend of the friend! I just wasn't ready to accept any or all invitations.

A Dating Scare

One particular experience brought it home to me very clearly that men getting back into the dating game also have problems. When a man I didn't know called me, I simply hung up the phone. It made me uncomfortable that he knew my name, where I lived, and how to reach me, while I didn't know him at all. I couldn't imagine where he had obtained this information.

The next night the same man called again, explaining that he had seen me at a restaurant in company with other women and decided he wanted to meet me. When I asked how he knew my phone number and name, he told me he had taken down my license-plate number as a way of obtaining the information. Now, that was frightening! I didn't know that such personal information was so readily available.

He went on to say that he was recently divorced and really did not know how to get acquainted with someone. I told him frankly that he had chosen a poor way to begin. When I acknowledged that he had frightened me, he said he hadn't realized the effect his approach would have on a woman living alone.

In fact, he turned out to be quite a nice man who knew some of the same people that I knew. I wished him luck in finding a girlfriend, realizing that the dating game can be very bewildering to a man who suddenly finds himself single after many years of marriage.

Dreams Of Love

Truly, I was wishing that I could have been interested in him or some of the other men I met. I envied people who had someone they could love and be happy with, because even though I kept very busy, I was also extremely lonely. I had a lot of love left to give to someone. I could only wonder sadly whether that part of my life had ended for good.

One day I sat down and listed all the qualities that I would want in a man. Looking over my list, I felt confident that it was a reasonable one.

Qualities I Would Want In A Man

1. A Christian and church-goer
2. A nice personality — cheerful
3. Either a college graduate or someone who was successful in his chosen vocation
4. Someone who enjoys sports and travel
5. Someone young enough to keep up with me — young at heart
6. Preferably a widower who had had a happy marriage
7. Kind and considerate to me and my family
8. Romantic — one who pursues me

Yet, knowing the statistics, I imagined I would be a widow for the rest of my life. Was that God's plan?

Claiming An Anchor

As church educational director, I wrote a weekly column for the church newsletter, but I hadn't settled on a name for my column. One morning I noticed that another staff member was drinking coffee from a mug that had an anchor design on the side. "That's it," I thought. "I'll call my column 'Anchored In Faith.' " As my trademark Scripture passage, I chose this:

> "Which hope we have as an anchor of the soul,
> both sure and steadfast . . . ."

> — Hebrews 6:19 (KJV)

I signed my column, "Anchored in Him." Thereafter the anchor symbol became very meaningful to me. Used as a noun, the word "anchor" means support, security, protection; as a verb, it means to secure firmly. For me, the anchor represents Christ and faith. And I especially liked the fact that in shape it is similar to a cross, the primary symbol of our Christian faith. I did indeed feel anchored in Christ — the only life support system that I knew I could count on.

By now my interim position was working out well, and my church activities proved very rewarding. I was thankful to have this opportunity for service. As no committee had been elected to search for a full-time educational director, I assumed that my work would continue there indefinitely. As my responsibilities grew, I was grateful for every bit of experience I gained.

Another Holiday Solution

As a widow, I had come to dislike Valentine's Day — the lovers' or sweethearts' special day for showing their love. I expected no Valentine cards, candy, or flowers myself, nor would there be a special romantic dinner invitation. Sadly, we take all these wonderful times for granted while our partners are alive, and then when they are gone . . . .

Imagining that the widows and widowers in our church family might feel as bereft as I around this special time, I decided to plan a non-Valentine banquet for all of us to enjoy. Even though the event was planned for February 14, I called it "The Midwinter Mystery Banquet."

Now, I had never been in charge of a banquet before, and I knew it would requie much preparation. I wanted the program to be funny and fun — something that would help people to laugh, let go, and really enjoy the occasion. I didn't want anyone to feel left out because they didn't have a spouse or "significant other." And because I had chosen the mystery theme, I decided to keep the program personalities a surprise.

How pleased I was with the outcome! We had a great crowd, our cooks did a marvelous job, and our speakers kept everyone laughing. Many of the older guests told me that they hadn't laughed that hard in years, and that they had left the banquet feeling so happy and so good. I was grateful that my initial effort turned out so well, encouraging me to tackle more such undertakings. God was again leading me forward, preparing me for similar occasions that would be an important part of my future work.

Like Valentine's Day, anniversaries, birthdays, and any other occasions that are special to a couple may evoke sadness and depression long after one's partner is gone. At the time that I was filling my first church position, I had been widowed for seven years. Am I delivering bad news by saying you may sometimes feel depressed years after your loss? Well, I prefer to call it reality. There will always be a few times when memories make you sad. And when those moments come, we have to be ready to meet them.

In the early years of my widowhood, on one of my visits to the cemetery, I encountered a woman who was tending her husband's grave. She had cleaned the headstone, attended to the plantings, and done everything possible to eliminate any indication of neglect.

When I asked how long her husband had been gone, she answered, "Ten years." Those words really dealt me a blow. Would I be doing the same thing myself, ten years after Paul's death?

Dealing With Depression

By now I was tired of grieving. I was tired of making all the decisions. I was tired of being alone. I was tired of not being special to any other person. I repeatedly asked myself, and God, whether my life would always be colored by this yearning for something or someone, and whether that something or someone was truly not in my future.

Friends have offered me various solutions for depression, all good. One older widow told me that whenever she felt depressed, she got out of the house and visited someone who needed a visit. I tried this method myself and can truthfully say that every time I used it, I ended up feeling better. It's nearly impossible to feel sorry for yourself when you are reaching out to another.

Whenever I got into one of these depressed moods, it helped me to write down all the feelings I was experiencing. You may also find that writing out your feelings helps. Writing about feelings is not something just for women. In my experience men often have difficulty telling another human being their painful feelings, and many men find writing these feelings out a help as well. Remember, no one ever has to see the words you put on paper except you.

Sometimes I wrote in the form of verse, sometimes in prose. I dated each page and gave it a title such as "Depression Page #1," "Depression Page #2," and so on. I am including Depression Page #1 here to let you know that all of us have these difficult times and can learn to move beyond them.

Depression Page #1

It is one of those rainy, bleak January days. The Christmas and New Year's activities are over. Gloom settles over me as I glance out to see evening ending the day. Why am I so despondent?

This year started out with much more promise than the one before. My financial situation was better; my health was good. Still, something was lacking. There has been no change as far as relationships are concerned. Life just stays the same, or even stagnates a little. I think about the expectations that I once had — now only a dream.

I had thought I was being called to give up teaching and prepare myself for a full-time religious vocation. Needless to say, there has been no full-time anything. I had hoped to use my teaching skills and work as a consultant at the Sunday School Board; I just "knew" that this was to be my calling. Was I deceiving myself? Isn't it strange how we get these ideas and think that they come from God? After all, if this had been God's will for my life, wouldn't it have worked out by now?

I guess I'm just a dreamer. I keep hoping things will change, that I will find companionship, yet seven and a half years have passed and I'm still very much alone. Oh, my life has been fulfilling in many ways, but I keep waiting — for what, I don't really know.

It's time to go home now. My little dog will be anxious to see me, the cat will be hungry, and there I will be — just me and the TV. The phone seldom rings, and then it's usually a wrong number, or someone trying to sell something. Don't you feel sorry for me? Well, you need not, because I'm sorry enough for myself. Funny, really, when most people think I am so happy.

Now, that's about as honest a portrait of self-pity as you could paint, isn't it? I knew it would do me no good to write such a page unless I was as frank as possible about my feelings. No one else was going to read it. The purpose was just to allow me to vent some of these unhappy feelings and gain relief by doing so. My Depression Pages served that purpose very well. Writing this passage must have made a difference for me, because months passed before I wrote another such page. And over the years the number of them gradually decreased until finally I had no need to write Depression Pages at all.

Having a friend with whom we can speak this honestly and openly is wonderful, but not everyone has such a friend, and in the absence of one, talking to ourselves in this way can help. I never intended for anyone to see these pages or read what my secret feelings were, but now I hope that my practice may also help you get in touch with your own feelings when things are not going so cheerfully.

Yet depression or no, I never completely lost my faith that God still had good things in store for me. It's true — God has good things in store for each and every one of us. Better days were in my future, and better days will also be in yours if you open yourself to the possibility and hold fast to your hope. God is always teaching us something about ourselves.

At one point I came across a quotation helpful for such times: "To know the road ahead, ask those coming back." Every town across this country has people who have known the heartbreak of losing a beloved partner, and many have found ways to handle their sorrow and move on. Finding such a person as a companion may be one of the best things you can do as you walk this road yourself.

Now, whenever I look in my notebook to see what I wrote on these various Depression Pages, I am happy to say that most of my fears and my sources of unhappiness have been eliminated — in God's own timing. Most of us are so convinced that we know what is best for us and when we should have it; yet all the while, God is working His purposes out in His own way and His own time.

A Day Of Contentment

On a summer morning months after my first Depression Page was written, I was sitting at my patio table enjoying some cold watermelon. Looking out into the woods, I could see squirrels chasing each other, birds enjoying the birdbath, and the cat so contented that she wasn't even a threat to the birds. And I found myself contented as well.

The phone rang, and I was delighted to hear the voice of Barbara, my seminary neighbor-friend, who was passing through town on her way to South Carolina. She was still working on her Ph.D. at the seminary, although she was finding life challenging as a student and widow with two children. We were able to have lunch together and said goodbye with hugs and hopes to meet again soon.

A week later, on her way home, Barbara called again to tell me about a ministry opportunity. She had attended a large church in the town where she was visiting and had learned that the minister to senior adults would be retiring the following year. Barbara insisted that I send my résumé in to this church right away and pressed me so hard that I told her I would do as she asked. Her friend was educational director at the church; perhaps that would help.

As I dropped my résumé in the mail, I entertained few hopes about the job. *I'm almost as old as the woman who is retiring. They will want someone with comparable experience who has been in another large church. They will probably hire a man anyway.* And that was the last I thought about the situation.

Keeping Spirits Up

I have found many ways to deal with my loneliness. One is to have something to look forward to, even if only dinner and a movie with a friend. Sometimes a friend and I would plan a shopping excursion, although the damage to my credit-card account was usually not worth the fleeting pleasure. Whatever makes you feel good is important.

When a Broadway play came to our town, my friend Ila and I bought tickets to see it, selecting seats on the third row. Mickey Rooney was the star, and we laughed from the time the curtain went up until the final curtain call. I hadn't laughed that much since the first day of my widowhood. Grief had become such a consistent part of my life that I found it a wonderful release just to laugh, uproariously.

A special treat came when the singles group at my former church invited me to join them on a weekend cruise to the Bahamas. I had never been on a cruise, and I had saved up enough money that I felt I could afford to go on this one. This trip was really something to look forward to. My anticipation of a great time was completely fulfilled by the reality. Now I would be braver about going on other group trips, even without a companion or a friend.

Another Social Venture

Just before leaving on the cruise I had received a phone call from a man I'll call Morris, who worked with my son-in-law. I had only spoken to him briefly when visiting my daughter, knowing very little about him. He was Jewish, that much I knew, and he told me he was divorced and wanted to fly down from New Jersey to see me. After exchanging a few letters and phone calls, I agreed to have him come.

Morris turned out to be a very interesting man, but I suspected he was wife-hunting for someone who would take care of him, and that certainly was not me. After seeing my lifestyle and involvements in church life and work, I sensed that his interest cooled; nevertheless, we had a very enjoyable weekend. He asked me many questions about my faith. It was a few weeks before Christmas, and my first date since the previous Christmas. Two dates in a year — not too bad for someone my age!

Even though I was flattered by this man's attention, I wrote it off as one more episode with no future, a knowledge that left me feeling depressed. Would there ever be anyone who was just right for me?

My interim work at church had been going well for a year and a half. As the New Year began, with three classes to teach at the community college, I was about to conclude that God must want me to be in part-time church work and part-time teaching. I had everything all figured out — or so I thought.

New Prospects

My daughter and son-in-law now told me they would be moving out of the apartment in my house to accept a job transfer to another city. I got busy and found a single person to come in in their place, but I was really lonesome after they left. I missed my family, although I was thankful that they had been there when I was most in need of their company and support.

Soon after they left I was surprised by another unexpected telephone call — this one from the chairman of a church committee in South Carolina, the same church to which I had sent a résumé at my friend Barbara's urging. Although it had been a long time since I had submitted that résumé, the committee was just beginning to go over all the applications they had received. Was I still interested in the position? Of course I was interested!

Having taught myself over the preceding few years to harbor scant expectations about church opportunities, I held out little hope even after this call. Other churches had corresponded with me, and I had filled out questionnaires and submitted untold numbers of résumés, but nothing ever came of any of these. But then the same committee chairman phoned again. He was so friendly and nice that I felt entirely at ease during our conversation. The committee wanted me to fly down, meet with them, and attend Sunday services. I was delighted to go and do as they requested. Was God working on my behalf?

Several of the committee members were to meet me at the airport; I told them to watch for the blonde wearing a white leather coat. They were there on time. Heightened security measures had called for everyone's luggage to be searched, with little effort made to repack properly. and when my suitcase arrived at the baggage claim area, half of my clothing was sticking out of the cracks. One of the ladies said, "I sure do like the way you pack!" We all laughed. The ice was broken.

That evening when I met with the full committee, I really felt that God was leading me in this new direction. Having known these people for just a few hours, I felt surrounded by a warmth and closeness that was remarkable. The work that had already been done in this church by the retiring minister with about 700 active senior adults was most impressive. Even though I sensed God's leading in this situation, at the same time I was scared. Could I really do the work? Could I live up to my predecessor's high standard? I knew it would be a great responsibility.

After returning home from this positive and encouraging visit, I knew the likelihood of a call was looming. I continued to pray about it, because I wanted to be sure this move would be an expression of God's will for my life. In terms of the job, I was concerned about budget planning, editing a newsletter, coordinating a pastoral ministry to 70 homebound persons, planning trips and programs, and all the rest. Fortunately the church had a large staff, with five other members, so I would have good staff support.

One of the fine things about committing Bible verses to memory in our youth is that they come back to nourish us in later years. Now a verse I had memorized as a young girl brought me courage: *"I can do everything through Him who gives me strength." (Phil. 4:13, NIV)*

Again this South Carolina committee called, inviting me for another weekend. Hearing that I was to be the guest of honor at a churchwide reception, I felt sure I would be offered the position. On the final Sunday evening I would know the decision. We had already discussed and agreed on such details as salary, benefits, moving expenses, and the like. What more was there to be said?

Faithfulness Rewarded

On Sunday night the favorable decision came. How happy I was! The new salary seemed incredibly generous. If I had continued teaching at the high school, even with a master's degree, I would never have made so much money. And the total compensation package was just great.

I had a great deal to do in preparation for my move. Knowing that I would be moving to smaller quarters, I placed a newspaper ad for everything I couldn't use, and what I didn't sell, I gave away. One of my friends commented that this part of the change was sad. Maybe it was sad to her, but it didn't seem sad to me. I felt like a butterfly bursting out of its cocoon, moving from one stage of life to claim a happier, greater one. I knew that when I moved from that house I would not be back.

Farewell To A Home

Ours had been a wonderful home, situated on 30 acres. When the children were growing up, each one had had a horse. The place was filled with memories of high-school kids, parties, horseback riding, and the "barn crowd," as the high-school students who boarded their horses with us called themselves.

When Paul was alive, the place had been beautifully kept, but I could never keep things the way he had done, and slowly everything had begun to look neglected. I could not afford to keep fences mended, fields cut, the house updated — all the things that need to be done around a place. Even if I had had the money, which I did not, finding someone reliable to help was always a problem.

When a buyer was found, turning the whole business over would be a considerable relief. I asked my realtor friend to take charge of renting my house with the possibility of selling it. That way I would have an income stream to cover the mortgage payment and essential repairs until a sale was worked out.

Moving On

I made arrangements to rent a suitable apartment in the new town, but it would not be available as soon as I needed it, so I was forced to take a small furnished apartment temporarily, until the one I had chosen was ready. So much to do, so many details to take care of.

Put yourself in my shoes, if you can. I was 61 years old — 61! — beginning a new career, moving to a town where I knew no one except the committee members I had met. I was leaving my family and friends and a home where I had lived for almost 30 years. Yet I was truly excited, for I knew that God had answered my prayers and was leading me in the direction He intended for me to go. Not everything would be a bed of roses, but God was making it easier for me to leave the past behind.

To my surprise, the church I was leaving gave me a wonderful going-away party. My time there had meant much to me, for with that congregation and staff I had learned much and gained much preparation for the work I was now going on to do. I felt a deep sense of gratitude for all I had gained there. In fact, every job that I had had during those three confusing years — the years when I often wondered what I was "supposed to" be doing, whether I was really moving in accordance with God's will, whether there would ever be an end to my anxieties — every job played some part as a training ground for me.

If we hold our hearts open to Him, God has much to teach us while we are in our waiting times. Even today, when I think about having been invited to fill that new position, I find it difficult to believe that they actually called me. But Scripture had already spoken to my disbelief:

> *"Jesus looked at them and said,*
> *'With man this is impossible, but not with God;*
> *All things are possible with God.' "*   — Mark 10:27

A Friend's Welcome Support

Knowing that my drive to the new place would take me through unfamiliar territory, and that I now had two small dogs to look after, my good friend Ila offered to accompany me to South Carolina. I probably wouldn't have asked her to do it, but I was truly grateful when she made the offer herself, even taking on the expense of flying back on her own. Eager to see the church and where I would be living, Ila wanted to share my new adventure in some way, for she was that kind of a friend. Such friends can never really know how much we appreciate their thoughtfulness and deep caring for us. As I packed up and made the final preparations, my thoughts took a poetic form that expressed my feelings well:

> *"I am moving my anchor*
> *Going on to explore*
> *The bountiful blessings*
> *God has in store.*
> *His guidance so clear*
> *And with nothing to fear,*
> *I move on."*

Part Four

New Light

He who deliberates fully
Before taking a step
Will spend his entire life on one leg.

— Chinese proverb

A Big Step

I deliberated little about the big new step I was about to take, for I had too many confirmations that it was the right thing to do. There would be obstacles to overcome, but I always drew on that heart-knowledge I had originally had when I first concluded that God was urging me to apply to the seminary to prepare for a new vocation.

When Ila and I arrived at the lovely town that was to become my new home, two female members of the selection committee were on hand to welcome us. Both widows themselves, they understood what it was like to go home to an empty house at the end of the day, and what it might be like to arrive as a stranger in an unfamiliar town. A certain camaraderie exists among widows, and I have had many occasions to be grateful for it. These new friends treated Ila and me to dinner, providing all of us with a good opportunity for getting to know one another.

Now I was to begin putting down roots in a new place, the first time I had done such a thing alone. Looking back, I marvel at my courage in undertaking such a drastic change. But then the years since Paul's death had seemed to be one long series of drastic changes.

One Step At A Time

Fortunately, when I made this move, I had no idea that there would be other drastic changes and other moves in the years ahead. Do you believe, as I do, that God gives us just as much information about our future as we need at the moment? In His mercy, he allows us to see just far enough to take the next step. If He were to lay out the whole future before us, plain to see, most of us would probably be so frightened that we couldn't move a big toe. No, He leads us step by step, day by day, and we are happiest when we learn to trust that His grace is sufficient.

To my relief, Ila volunteered to stay on with me for a few more days while I took up my new church responsibilities. She helped arrange for my utilities and locate a bank, a dog kennel, the hospitals (I knew already I would have visitation responsibilities), and, of course, the mall! The final necessity, a beautician, was one I had already taken care of myself, so everything was covered. Or so I thought.

My new job was both exciting and frightening. Self-doubts surfaced again. Could I do this job? Could I follow in the footsteps of my excellent predecessor? I knew very little about planning an organizational budget, arranging trips, producing a newsletter. I had so much to learn. But Scripture came to my rescue: *"For nothing is impossible with God." (Luke 1:37, NIV).* When I came across that encouraging word, it was as if God was saying to me, "Jane, you have a short memory. You haven't done a thing *on your own* yet."

After taking Ila to the airport and finding myself alone again, homesickness tried to wash over me, but I banished it after a minute or two. I had prayed and waited for this opportunity for such a long time, and I knew this was the place God had been preparing me for and preparing for me. This calling was God's will for me at that time in my life — of that I was sure.

The Wrong Foot

I shall never forget my first Sunday in my new position. Naturally, anyone in a new place and among new people is eager to make a good impression, particularly if those people are responsible for signing your paycheck. On that first Sunday I was ready especially early, for I was to attend both services to be introduced and received as a new member of the church.

After I closed and locked the door of the apartment and went out to my car, I was horrified, for there, lying on the front seat of my *locked* car, was my only set of car keys. I hadn't missed them because they were separate from the apartment key. I had no phone yet, and it was very early on Sunday morning. What in the world was I to do?

After wandering around the apartment complex in hope of finding someone awake, I finally found one apartment with signs of activity, and the kind tenant allowed me in to use her phone. When she spotted me at 8:00 A.M. all dressed up with a big Bible in one hand, she probably concluded she was in for a missionary talk. How thankful I was that she was willing to help me out of the fix I had created for myself.

Yet I should not have been surprised that such a thing had happened, because under stress we are more apt to behave in uncharacteristic ways. My underlying feelings of homesickness and loneliness, worry about the unfamiliar environment, the new job, making the right impression — all these added up to tremendous stress at that time. Even though I was embarrassed to admit what had happened, I telephoned the chairman of the selection committee — the only phone number I happened to have. Fortunately, his wife answered just as she was leaving for church, and she graciously offered to pick me up and drive me there.

How insecure I felt arriving at the church that morning! I found it difficult to concentrate on the services, knowing I would still have to find someone to help me get into my car afterward. Would the church folk think me careless and stupid? Maybe I was, but I didn't want them to find it out on my first day among them.

Helpful Resources

For anyone who needs help in crises such as locking your keys in the car or a flat tire, I recommend joining one of the various travel plans or automobile associations. I already had such a membership, and when I called someone came quickly and took care of the situation. Gone are the days when most of us can open a locked car door with a coat hanger. Having had dead batteries, flat tires, and various other car problems, I'm extremely grateful that I can just pick up the phone and call, knowing that someone will be there shortly to help. Whatever gives you a sense of security is good.

Getting My Feet Wet

The second weekend of my new employment I was on call. This meant that I wore a beeper and was to respond if there was any emergency. The rest of the staff had reassured me that any call would be very unlikely. Wrong! I was at home unpacking boxes when the call came. A man had died, and I was wanted at the family's home immediately. I arrived to discover that the new widow was a woman who had gone visiting homebound members with me only a few days earlier. Now she was in distress, and I was the one who had come in answer to the call.

I felt so helpless! I wished that I knew what to do or say that would help her, although just being there was about as much as I had to offer at the moment. I did remember to call the senior pastor's secretary, who promised that the pastor would be there soon. In spite of my own feelings of inadequacy, I knew that a pastor's presence is often a great comfort to family members at such times.

I also knew that in the days ahead this widow would need me more than in the immediate crisis, and I planned to be there for her. I could never forget my own desolation, emptiness, and inability to be consoled. I vowed to do all I could to reach out to her and all the other widows and widowers among my new friends.

My work soon brought me into contact with many such persons. Other staff members always liked to tease me about the widowers, but I had learned not to let such teasing bother me. If we are psychologically healthy, the desire for companionship is natural. Furthermore, such good-natured teasing is generally a sign that the ones doing the teasing like the person teased. I took it as a compliment and let it go at that.

Another Try At Dating

After I got moved into my "permanent" apartment, within a few weeks the apartment manager asked if I would consider meeting another single tenant who was very lonesome. Concluding that it must be time for Date #3, I said I would. Soon afterward, when I was out walking my dogs, a man came up and introduced himself, saying he would like me to have dinner with him soon. A pleasant enough person, he told me he was divorced. Well, we would see.

When our dinner date came about, both of us must have felt the absence of any electricity between us, for we were back home before dark. Experience had taught me to entertain no unrealistic expectations, but I think my escort may have been a bit let down.

Still Not Settled In

After a couple of months in that apartment, I became dissatisfied, for I had discovered other tenants — little crawling ones — that nothing would deter. Once again, I started looking for a better place. I had noticed some particularly attractive condominiums nearby and soon discovered that some of our church members lived there. When they heard I was interested, they told me about a unit for rent and even gave me the out-of-state owners' phone number. When I called, they readily accepted me as a new renter, two dogs and all. The cost was very little more than what I was already paying, and I could handle it financially. God is so good!

Dreading the physical labor of moving again so soon after my last move, when I told the maintenance man at the church about my predicament, he enlisted a couple of the men of the church and found a truck to move the heavy furnishings. With the help of some of the church women I had already moved dishes, clothes, pictures and the like. Soon I was settled again, and I really loved the new place.

Yet Another Holiday

The Fourth of July came. I attended a local celebration and crafts fair, but when I returned to my condo with a long blank holiday weekend ahead of me, that old homesick feeling washed over me again. Memories swam up of countless Fourth of July celebrations back in Tennessee. Out whole family had always gone on a picnic. The Great Smoky Mountains were beautiful, and we reveled in the cool mountain springs and creeks, spending the entire day in the glorious outdoors — always having a wonderful time. I was missing my family and friends, familiar places, and the house where I had lived for so long. I wished I could simply skip the holidays — any holidays.

I dealt with that homesickness after a bit, when I felt confident enough about my work to take a few days off for a trip back. I had dreaded making the drive alone, but learning that the pastor's secretary had a sister who lived in my hometown, I invited her to go along with me. She accepted happily, and I drove and dropped her off at her sister's house, then visited my own family. With God's help, things do work out. We just have to be open to the possibilities all around us.

Humor Helps

As I went about my work with the senior adults, some days were easy, while others were tough. At unexpected times, thank the Lord, comedy cropped up to lighten what might have been a dreary situation. On one of my nursing-home visits I was walking down the hall and had to pass a group of elderly men sitting around a table talking. Greeting them cordially, I commented on the beautiful day.

One of the men observed, "You have real pretty hair."

"Thank you," I replied, "but it really needs fixing."

"Yes," he said, "a little combing and brushing would help."

Talk about freedom of speech! The very elderly say what they please and couldn't care less what anyone thinks. Perhaps that is something we can all look forward to in our old age.

On another occasion, I was visiting two elderly women who shared a room. As we sat talking, a little old man came wheeling himself in, uninvited. Those two women got as mad as hornets. They really told that little old man where he could go. I didn't think the man's intentions were dishonorable, but I couldn't convince the two women to take a more charitable view. Maybe they knew something that I didn't know.

I had another shock when a certain elderly man telephoned me from the nursing home, saying he just wanted to talk. He asked me how I felt, and I replied, "Just fine. How are you feeling?"

"I sure would like to feel you!" was his astonishing reply. I was later told that in his younger years he had been a notorious ladies' man. Our same old selves are still there inside these aging bodies, frequently very thinly disguised. I suspect that what we were once, that we are forever.

Confidence And Optimism

By the end of my first year on the job, I thought I had my responsibilities pretty well under control. During that time I had simply implemented plans already made, but in the coming year my ministry would be entirely up to me. Because of my inexperience in some areas, I chose three of my senior adults to help me plan and estimate our budget. The officers of our senior-adult club also helped plan upcoming programs.

Staff support was extremely helpful. My secretary did many necessary things for me, and I really appreciated her. Getting out a monthly newsletter, teaching a weekly Bible class, carrying on visitation to 70 homebound members — I had a great deal of support for all these activities.

I enumerate these things to demonstrate two truths:

1. We are never too old to learn new things, provided we are willing to try, and

2. God provides people to help us when we commit ourselves to important tasks.

Singles And Couples

Although many in our senior-adult group were couples, I was greatly impressed by the contributions single and widowed persons were making to their community and to the church as volunteers. They were living very useful lives, keeping cheerful, full of energy. I admired them very much. One of these widows, who had lost not only her husband but also a son and daughter-in-law, remained busy and cheerful, volunteering for many duties at the church, visiting homebound people and nursing homes, and shining as the life of the party on many of our bus trips.

I also had to watch, sadly, as more of my senior adults lost their life partners and became widowed. Some who had seemed very strong to me were suddenly weak. Others whom I thought would have a very difficult time making it alone truly surprised me, showing a great deal of strength. I found it quite painful to watch people whom I had come to love suffer and die. As the months passed, many good people who at one time had made a big difference in my life now were no longer around.

Comfort In Sorrow

Praying by the bedside of a dying person is a very hard thing to do, yet I had to do it, knowing that we frequently derive our greatest comfort from prayer. Attending many funerals in the course of my work, I sometimes found my own sorrowful memories returning on these occasions, even though I also knew from personal experience that there would be better days ahead — yes, better days ahead — for these dear people.

Something To Rejoice About

Good and happy days surely outnumbered the sad ones. For the first time in years, I could afford to buy that all-American toy, a new car. Church friends told me of a car dealer, a fellow church member, who would be a good, honest person to see. My predecessor in my job had become a close friend, and since she knew him well and had bought her own car from him, I asked her to go along with me to shop for my new car. My choice of vehicle may have surprised her, however. I had always wanted a convertible — yes, at my age! If you don't get what you want when you are free to choose, when will you ever get it? I bought a beautiful white convertible, just what I needed to do all my visiting in.

Young At Heart

You will never catch me apologizing for being young at heart. I aim to think young and act young, stopping short (I hope) of appearing foolish. (I don't want to be like the woman another elderly woman described as "mutton all dressed up as lamb.") We must never let age keep us from doing whatever we want to do or feel like doing, provided it is respectable and within the bounds of good taste. In addition, I never let age keep me from wearing whatever I feel like wearing.

My approach to life is consistent with my goal in ministry with seniors: to make sure that we all have fun. Laughter and humor are good for us! There is nothing unChristian about enjoying life. In fact, many people want nothing to do with a Christian who always wears a gloomy face.

I worked hard to plan programs that would be uplifting and enjoyable, programs the seniors would look forward to. I did my best to plan pleasurable and exciting trips, for many of the women would never have had the opportunity to go on such trips if it were not for the opportunities offered through the church. Men who no longer wanted to drive could enjoy a vacation as well. I readily admit that we went to more shows than we did to museums. We wore jeans on the bus — none of this dressed-up stuff for us. Some younger church members finally tacked a comical label on us: S.I.D.s — Seniors In Denial!

Although these trips were a part of my work, I looked forward eagerly to every one. Like many of the other participants, I was able to go places and do things I had never dreamed of doing. We took two cruises together — one to the Bahamas and one to Hawaii. Did I have a great job, or what?

Many times on our trips things happened that added to everyone's fun. On one trip, some of the travelers were teasing me about the bus driver, saying that I probably intended to pair up with him. I laughed right along with them, taking their teasing no more personally than I had all the teasing about potential partners from others over the years. But the biggest laugh came when we arrived at the hotel and went to our rooms only to discover that my luggage had accidentally been put into the same room with his.

Jokes are life-enhancing. Laughter is good!

Community Builds Fulfillment

If you belong to a church where people feel wanted and included, valued and appreciated, you know what a wonderful role that church plays in your life and the lives of others. Affiliation with such a faith community has been a vital part of life for me, always. If your church isn't like that, perhaps you can look around and find one that is.

And even if you are not an active member of a church, the world around us offers many, many ways by which we can make useful contributions to our society. Before I went into full-time church work, I knew I was making useful contributions through my volunteer efforts, teaching in community colleges and adult literacy classes, on the riverboat cruises, and even during my short time in the children's day-care program. In every case, when I reached out to others, I myself was bountifully blessed. Of course at times I was also well and truly tired, but every day brought me some blessing or another, and I tried to keep my eyes open to recognize them.

Christianity Can Be Merry

In sharing appropriate activities with other Christians, I believe with all my heart that we are meant to look beyond those activities that are merely staid, earnest, and dull. The good news of the Gospel should bring us joy! We know from the Scripture accounts that Jesus often joined with his friends in parties and celebrations. People even accused some of Jesus' first followers of being drunk, because they were having such an uproarious good time. Obviously I am not advocating that we Christians behave like a bunch of drunks, but I believe with all my heart in finding occasions to celebrate and be happy together.

Recapturing the joys of life is all the more important as we age. Although we do have to accept certain diminishments that come with advancing years, a diminished joy of fellowship with other Christians is one we should never resign ourselves to. In my work with the senior adults, I arranged many banquets, holiday parties, and interesting programs for them to enjoy. Often, if no other speaker had been invited, I would give a little talk at these events myself. I always tried to make my remarks upbeat and cheerful, with an inspiring message of some sort at their core.

Planning one Christmas banquet for our widows and widowers, I wondered what I could do or say that would add to their enjoyment of the season. The year before, I had attended a similar event at which the evening's speaker was totally lacking in an understanding of the grief that recurs with holidays when we have lost someone we love. Instead of leaving that banquet with a joyous feeling, many of those present, including me, had gone home feeling sad.

This time I prayed for God to lead me in my preparations. I want to share here a summary of my talk for that evening, hoping these simple thoughts may bring you new encouragement and hope:

Christmas Secrets, Christmas Gifts

When my children were small, in the weeks before Christmas I always hid things in the closet so that my children wouldn't find them. We can all remember when the weeks before Christmas meant keeping secrets — good secrets.

Tonight, I have some secrets that may not be so good — secrets that I intend to put in my "closet" and leave there once and for all. These are secrets that truly need to be hidden if I am to find pleasure in the holidays and every other day.

- *This first package is labeled SELF-PITY. This is one box that should be hidden as far back in the closet as possible, so that no one will know that I have such a thing. For if others know I feel sorry for myself, they will feel less than happy themselves, and both of us will suffer.*

- *The second package is labeled AILMENTS. No matter how much I would like to tell people about my ailments, no one really wants to listen to such dreary accounts. I resolve to keep this box well hidden, too.*

- *The third box is labeled **LONELINESS**. Don't I need to let people know how lonely I feel? If they know, they may feel sorry for me. But nobody wants to be pitied. I've decided to keep that third box hidden, way in back next to the first two.*

- *The fourth box is a big one — **INDECISION**. I can't help fretting at times, because I get so tired of having to make all the decisions by myself. What if I make a wrong decision, or make it too soon, or too late? No one can answer such questions. We just have to do our best and go on. So I shove that box to the back of the closet as well.*

- *The fifth box, **DEPRESSION,** is one I surely don't want to display. Oh, yes, I know that if I am suffering a long-lasting depression that never lifts, I deserve and need professional help. But if I'm just having an occasional "bad" day, I don't have to let it take over my life. People don't like being around someone who's depressed and won't take steps to get better. I've decide to share my "blue" days only with a close friend who understands and leave it at that.*

- *But then, as I am hiding all these secret boxes in the back of my "closet," I also come across some other boxes that I have forgotten about. One that looks rather old and neglected is labeled **SWEETS**. Oh, yes, sweet memories! This is one that definitely needs to come out. I resolve to put it in a prominent place to help me remember the special Christmases of the past, the joyful times. Yes, I will occasionally enjoy my sweet memories, while recognizing that living only in the past is as unhealthy as eating too many sweets.*

- *Here's another box that needs to come out again — **LAUGHTER**. It's been a long time since I've enjoyed a hearty laugh, yet laughter is good for the soul. The Bible even tells us that. And so I resolve to do whatever I can to make laughter a part of my Christmas again, a part of every day.*

- *This last package is one that most certainly needs to stay outside the closet throughout the year — **THE GIFT OF LOVE**. This is truly a miraculous gift, for it is one that I can both keep and give away! No matter how much love I offer to others,* *more will always come back to me. Love is what Christmas is really all about — the Gift of Love that God gave us in the form of a tiny baby — Jesus. This Gift suits everyone: young and old, widows, widowers, women and men. It is the perfect gift for a happy Christmas. It is the gift that lasts a lifetime and beyond.*

After the banquet ended, many of those who took part came telling me that they had either hidden, or were now determined to hide, the very same things that I mentioned, and were going home inspired to bring out the things I had reminded them of that they could cherish. They were smiling and happy. And I was happy, too.

Many times during my journey through and beyond grief, I found it helpful to put my thoughts into the form of simple poems. I make no claims to being a poet, but maybe my expressions will speak to you also.

Lighten Your Load

Get rid of that baggage!
Lighten your load!
The weight of despair
Should be first to go.

Self-pity, there's no room for that.
What else? Complaining,
demanding, self-seeking and pride.
All of these you cast aside.

And over life's wall
You will fly as a dove
On the wings of contentment,
joy, and love,
soaring high and looking above.
It's easy when you
Lighten the load.

At Peace With Myself

As time went by, my social life improved. I had new friends, unmarried ones, with whom I could go places, and one of those places was to the Masters Golf Tournament. What a thrill that was! Again, it was an event I had seen on television, never dreaming I could watch it in person.

My two closest widow friends from home continued to come every summer to pay me a visit. Eventually we grew brave enough to undertake vacations together. I drove, and my friends read the road maps. People probably smiled when they saw three old ladies enjoying the trip in my convertible — good! I'm glad they did. We didn't feel old, and we were having fun. I could look back with relief now to the times when I was first widowed and afraid to stay out after dark. Our houses can become prisons to us, if we allow our fears to rule our lives.

I had come such a long way. Now I had security in my job at the church and enjoyed opportunities to make many new friends. I had learned to be comfortable around men and enjoy joking with them in a light-hearted way. Nevertheless, I was content to remain as I was — single.

My life was fine. I was managing my finances well. I could travel back and forth on the interstate highways by myself. I could take vacations with my friends, and the senior adults in our church had become my "family." Life was good. I had just about concluded that I would never marry again, and that was all right. When friends inquired, I told them it would probably take a miracle of God for a man ever to come into my life again.

The Teacher Is Taught

Although in my church work I was nominally the "teacher," I found early on that the senior adults with whom I worked every day could teach me a great deal about life. I continued learning from them that if you see life as a journey — a journey all of us are taking — you realize that age doesn't count.

Attitude is what matters. When energy faltered, I saw persistence succeed in its place. When the physical beauties of youth faded, I saw kindness produce beauty of a far more spiritual sort. When fear sought to dominate, I saw prayer brought in to win the day. I saw the power in faith, the power in hope, the tremendous power of unselfish love. I saw time cherished, and wise maturity crowning learning through life's mistakes. What was the sum of this priceless process? Happiness and contentment all around me, in people who had every reason not to feel happy or content.

In an admonition that we call the Golden Rule, Jesus told his followers, *"Do unto others as you would have them do unto you" (Matt. 7:12, KJV).* What better rule could there be for our golden years? It is the best rule for any age, regardless of the mileage we cover along life's journey.

In addition to the Golden Rule, I often tell my senior adult groups not to forget about their "Triple A Card": **Attitude, Action,** and **Achievement** for God's glory. With three such watchwords to guide us, how can any of us go wrong?

Scriptural Promises For Times Of Waiting And Anxiety

(All passages are all taken from the New International Version of the Bible.)

Be strong and courageous. Do not be afraid or terrified . . . . for the Lord your God goes with you; He will never leave you nor forsake you. (Deuteronomy 31:6)

You will keep in perfect peace him whose mind is steadfast, because he trusts in you. Trust in the Lord forever, for the Lord, the Lord, is the Rock eternal. (Isaiah 26:3)

The Lord is the everlasting God, the Creator of the ends of the earth. He will not grow tired or weary . . . . He gives strength to the weary and increases the power of the weak. Even youths grow tired and weary, and young men stumble and fall; but those who hope in the Lord will renew their strength. They will soar on wings like eagles; they will run and not grow weary, they will walk and not faint. (Isaiah 40:29-31)

When you pass through the waters, I will be with you; and when you pass through the rivers, they will not sweep over you. When you walk through the fire, you will not be burned; the flames will not set you ablaze. For I am the Lord, your God, the Holy One of Israel, your savior. (Isaiah 43:2-3)

Do not be anxious about anything, but in everything, by prayer and petition, with thanksgiving, present your requests to God. And the peace of God, which transcends all understanding, will guard your hearts and your minds in Christ Jesus. (Philippians 4:6-7)

My God will meet all your needs according to His glorious riches in Christ Jesus. (Philippians 4:19)

If any of you lacks wisdom, he should ask God, who gives generously to all without finding fault, and it will be given to him. (James 1:5)

. . . . I am with you always, even to the end of the world. (Matthew 28:20)

Part Five

At Last, Delight

*"Delight yourself in the Lord
and He will give you the desires of your heart."*

— *Psalms 37:4 (NIV)*

Blessings Abound

As I looked back over my first two years ministering with seniors, I felt very blessed by the experiences we had shared together. I had visited many states and seen many interesting sights. Niagara Falls, the Pennsylvania Amish people and country, Walt Disney World, Epcot, the New England states, Charleston in South Carolina, Opryland Hotel at Christmas, and New York were just some of our destinations.

I was privileged to teach a weekly Bible class that called for intensive study on my part, which was very good for me. My health was excellent, and I would soon celebrate my 65th birthday. I felt very blessed.

Another Dislocation

However, the condo I was renting was to be sold. I had been told of this probability and knew it would be shown to prospective buyers. While I was on a weekend cruise with my senior adults, a buyer turned up, and I had just two weeks to find another place to live. I couldn't blame the owners, because I still owned and rented out my house in Tennessee, and I knew how the expenses could add up.

Places to rent in our town were scarce, even scarcer for pet owners. I finally found a nice, practically new house in a small town nearby. Again, I had to call on my friends to help me move. This was my third move, but they were ever-patient and gracious. One couple had helped me hang mirrors and pictures so often that they knew exactly where I would want them. The men who did the heavy lifting were just thankful that I was finally moving into a place on the ground floor. I don't know how I could have moved that many times without the help of these dear friends. God always provides whom and what we need.

More Remedies For Loneliness

You may wonder why I held onto my two little dogs, for they surely did complicate things. For one thing, I had to leave them in a kennel while I was away on trips, which meant added expense, but to my mind they were worth it. My loneliness had never entirely gone away, and for anyone who lives alone, a pet of some sort is good for your health. They love you no matter how old you are. The later you are, the gladder they are to see you. They're always there to welcome you, and besides that, they give you a good excuse to talk to yourself. I remember one widower telling me that his dog was the only reason he had to get up in the mornings. Sometimes we do need a reason.

At the end of a longer-than-usual mission trip to Mexico that I took with a group from another church, when we arrived back in town late one evening, I noticed that all the other travelers were being met by someone special. I felt a tinge of loneliness — no one was there to meet me. For anyone who is alone again after having had a partner, times will come when being alone saddens you. Yet such feelings only last a little while, and then the sadness lifts. Many times my children welcomed me home by the modern invention of answering machines. I always appreciated their thoughtfulness. Even if my welcome was a recorded voice inside a machine, at least it was another human voice.

When my 65th birthday rolled around, I had no plans to retire. I intended to work as long as I had the opportunity of doing so. What would retirement have meant to me? I had no one at home, and I didn't have to look forward to "the good life." I was already there!

Holiday Milestones

As the Christmas season drew near, at last I bought a "real" tree and enjoyed decorating it. I loved the privacy of my new place, and a house just seemed more of a home to me than the apartments or condo where I had lived before. As to Christmas itself, I spent the holiday with my family in Tennessee. But when New Year's Eve rolled around, I found myself back in my own place alone, wondering what the new year would bring. Did I really believe I was alone? None of us is ever really alone, for God is always with us.

Even so, there are many times when I am like the little girl who was frightened of thunderstorms. One night as the lightning flashed and the thunder roared, her preacher daddy came in to reassure her.

"Stay with me, Daddy," she begged. "I'm scared!"

"Don't be afraid, honey," he comforted. "You know God is always with us."

"I know, Daddy," she wailed. "But right now I need somebody with some skin on them!"

There are many times when we just plain need another human being with us for comfort and companionship. God understands. After all, He sent His Son to dwell among us.

On the second day of the new year, I was taking down my Christmas decorations when the phone rang. The telephone has had a great deal to do with life-changing opportunities for me. Surely God can work through the telephone on our behalf! This time I was happily surprised to hear the voice of Anna, a former neighbor whom I had not seen in 10 years. She and her husband Cal had been friends of mine for many years and were now living in Georgia. When Paul died they had come, and we had kept in touch afterwards. Real friends do that.

After we caught up on all our family news, she told me that she hoped I could help with a situation in which she felt inadequate. Knowing that my work often required me to deal with bereavement, she needed my advice. A dear friend had recently lost his wife and was having a very difficult time. She wanted to help him but didn't know how. Did I know of a book or other resource that she could give him? This man's wife had also been Anna's best friend, and the two couples had spent much time together. After the wife's death, they still went out to eat together, bowled together on the church bowling team, and sat together in church, but suddenly now they were a threesome, not a foursome, and everything seemed out of kilter.

Without knowing it, Anna was already helping that friend, for just being there is all-important. Immediately after the funeral and in the next few weeks when people begin dropping away is when the loneliness really sets in. There are no easy answers, no remedies that will remove all of the pain, but phone calls, cards, and invitations to share meals or outings mean the world when we are left alone. Hugs are also good!

I told Anna I would send her a book to give him. As we ended our conversation, she said, "At some time I'd like the two of you to meet." When I returned to work I chose a small paperback book that I had given to other grieving people and mailed it to her.

Unusual Developments

I thought no more about our conversation until a Sunday evening a few weeks later when Anna called again. Their friend, Boyce, was at their house at that very moment, and she wanted me to speak to him.

I was truly embarrassed. We were strangers. I didn't know what to say, and he was as much at a loss as I, because he hadn't even known who it was that Anna had been speaking to. Awkwardly, we introduced ourselves and briefly spoke. I did notice what a nice voice he had. I was glad he had the friendship of these people who had been such dear friends to me. Later Anna told me she had explained to him that I had gone through the same experience, losing my husband, and telling him about my background and my church work.

The Church Lady

One factor had a great deal to do with my feeling that I would probably never marry again — my discovery that most men just were not interested in a woman in church work. They seemed to have preconceived notions that such a woman would be different from the "normal" woman to the extent that she wouldn't ever think of sex, or that, if she did, it wouldn't be very important to her. Sometimes I wonder where these ideas come from.

In subsequent conversations Anna told me more about Boyce, but I was only mildly curious. I imagined that, as fast as the world moves today, the next time I talked to her, he would have remarried. In my experience, most men can't stay single for long.

Again, the telephone. God bless Alexander Graham Bell! Several days after our introduction by phone, my phone rang again just after I had come from church and Sunday lunch with friends.

"Hello, Jane. This is Boyce Jones. Remember we spoke to each other on the phone while I was visiting Cal and Anna?"

"This is who?" Was I playing it cautious, afraid to appear too interested?

He wanted to talk about his bereavement and loneliness, problems I could surely identify with. I too knew what it was like to lose your lover and dearest friend on earth. Boyce and his wife June had been married for 42 years when she died from breast cancer. My husband Paul and I had been married 33 years when he died. Even though I had been a widow for almost 13 years by then, I certainly had not forgotten the pain and anxiety. You really never forget. It simply gets easier to bear. I told him to call me any time he wanted to talk. And he had such a nice voice.

Boyce's way of dealing with his grief truly impressed me, for he was doing it in a very healthy manner. He was acknowledging it, expressing it, reaching out for help, allowing tears, and accepting "feeling bad." These were good signs — signs that he was allowing himself to go deeply into his loss in order that he might eventually move beyond it to rediscover life.

Keeping Quiet

I didn't mention this phone call to anyone at my church, my friends, or my children. The only person I told was Anna. Boyce had already spoken to her, saying that I was very easy to talk to, which made me feel good. I had begun wondering whether God just "might be" in this situation. In one way I was beginning to be interested, and in another way I wasn't. I was afraid to hope for too much. Boyce continued to call me, and we both looked forward to these talks.

Then Anna decided that I must come for a visit in order to meet Boyce in person. She told me she was sure he was more than a little interested in me. She had shown him my picture (not a close-up, fortunately). But in the next two months I had a great deal of travel scheduled — to Hawaii with one group, then a convention at Myrtle Beach, followed by a conference in Colorado. A trip to Atlanta would be difficult to fit in.

Feeling Drawn

Yet Anna's invitation kept pulling at me. I had taken no vacation time in the new year, because my senior-adult trips were all working trips. I decided that I could take one day of vacation on a Sunday, and since I was off every Friday and Saturday anyway, I targeted the St. Patrick's Day weekend to drive to Atlanta.

Before I went, my daughter and son-in-law came for a visit, and while they were there I had a postcard and another call from Boyce.

I figured it was time to tell them about this brew that was warming up, although they seemed to attach little importance to it. The next person I told was my secretary. We had become very close friends, and I knew I could confide in her. I told her about my phone calls and intended trip, and she was very excited for me. I made her promise not to mention this news to anyone.

Boyce and I continued our telephone conversations and exchanged cards. I could tell that he was a very thoughtful person. He had been to Hawaii himself, so we discussed my upcoming trip; we also discussed our families and our church activities and friends. I was glad to know that he was a Christian and that some of his best friends had been pastors. I still had no idea of his appearance. Anna had told me that he was nice-looking, but we all say that about many people.

When our seniors group left for Hawaii, we traveled by bus to the Atlanta airport to board our plane. Nearing the city, I noticed a particular restaurant and filed this location away in my mind as a potential future meeting place. I figured I could get myself to this point with no difficulty, but I certainly did not want to drive in the Atlanta traffic.

Our Hawaiian trip was marvelous. We boarded a cruise ship to tour the various islands. Several couples were celebrating anniversaries. Most of my group were couples, with just a few widows. Hawaii is such a romantic place! I told my group that if ever I went back there again, I would take a man with me even if I had to pay him. They all enjoyed the joke. We had a wonderful time.

It is a tradition in Hawaii that if you want to return there again, you must throw your lei into the wake of the ship as you depart. When I tossed my lei into the water, the wind blew it back onto the deck. Was this a bad omen? Time would tell.

Arriving back in Atlanta after the long flight, our group boarded the bus for the wearisome ride the rest of the way home. I made no phone calls as we passed through. I was eager to get home, talk to my family, and repack for the upcoming trip to Myrtle Beach.

The convention there lasted three days, during which the upcoming trip to Atlanta really began to invade my thoughts. I took advantage of free time to walk the beach and collect my thoughts. It was great just to walk along and enjoy the ocean's peace.

A Momentous Meeting

Boarding the bus for home again, I knew I had to prepare in earnest for the visit to Anna and Cal and meeting with Boyce. "Mixed feelings" is an apt description of me as we covered the last miles. My life up to that point had become settled and relatively uncomplicated, and I liked it that way. One of the positive things about being alone is that all decisions affect just one person — you. I was trying to manage my feelings with composure, but I was not eager to travel back to Atlanta again.

At home, I found a vase with one red rose waiting for me. The card read, "Only one day left until we meet. Boyce." This man had a very sentimental side — and I liked it and was touched.

Remembering the restaurant I had picked out as a possible meeting place, I called and asked Cal and Anna to ask if they would drive there and meet me on the morning of my arrival, which they were happy to do. I just hoped my knees wouldn't be knocking when I got out of the car.

When I called each of my children to tell them where I would be staying, my younger daughter's remark took me aback: "Mom, it's going to be a very long weekend if you discover that you don't like this man." All the same, I trusted that I had been led thus far and would step out in faith the rest of the way. I repacked my old suitcase, including a Blarney Stone souvenir that I had bought in Savannah on a previous St. Patrick's Day that would make a timely gift.

Next morning, leaving home at 8:00 A.M., doubts again assailed me. *I don't need this. I'm happy the way I am. What if he doesn't like me? What if I don't like him? Why didn't I keep this relationship limited to the telephone wires?* Half an hour away from our meeting place I pulled into a rest stop, troubled thoughts whirling through my mind. Perhaps I should just turn around and go back home.

But my friends had gone to no little trouble to arrange this weekend for me. Would I be so inconsiderate as to refuse to carry it through? Anna's and Cal's friendship meant more to me than that. And I really did want to meet Boyce — my telephone friend with the nice, nice voice. I resolved to make the best of whatever the situation might bring. I had already been praying about it for a month and more.

Wrapped up in myself and my own feelings, I never stopped to think that Boyce and my friends were probably as anxious as I.

My tardy arrival must have added to their concern. Driving those last few miles, I remembered the Old Testament story I had read days before of how Abraham sent his servant to a far country to find a wife for his son Isaac. Knowing that the servant should soon return with the bride-to-be, Isaac was out in the field meditating. *"As he looked up,"* the Scripture reported, *"he saw camels approaching. Rebekah also looked up and saw Isaac. She got down from her camel and asked the servant, 'Who is that man in the field coming to meet us?' "* (Genesis 24:13-65, NIV). The beautiful story had ended with Rebekah becoming Isaac's beloved wife. That was one blind date with a happy ending. I prayed my meeting would turn out half so well.

My welcoming committee was certainly keeping a sharp eye out for me, for by the time I had parked the car, my friends stood beside it. We exchanged hugs, and then a man's voice — a nice voice — said, "May I have a hug too?" I looked up to see a tall, very handsome man. It was Boyce. I was delighted to meet him at last. Yes, I did give him that hug.

The Brew Begins To Boil

Our brunch went well. I felt very comfortable sitting beside this man, for we had already shared some of our deepest feelings, our times of greatest vulnerability and need. How could we not have felt a bond?

When we left the restaurant, Boyce said to me, "Aren't you glad that's over?" I laughed. "I surely am." I handed him my car keys, and he drove on following Cal and Anna to Atlanta. Our conversation continued to flow naturally and spontaneously. The weekend was off to a very promising start.

At Cal's and Anna's house, a vase of beautiful red roses stood waiting for me, with a card that read, "Here are the other eleven. Welcome to Atlanta. Boyce." This man certainly knew how to make someone feel special. I was coming to see him as the kind of gracious, thoughtful Southern gentleman I had often admired in the movies but rarely was fortunate enough to meet in real life.

After a day of sightseeing and visiting interesting places, we four went out to dinner, then to the mall, and to a movie. It was a full day, and I was having a very good time except for one thing. At mealtimes, I couldn't eat. Why would someone who generally loves eating suddenly be unable to force more than a few bites down? Boyce was having no difficulty with his appetite. Well, different strokes for different folks.

At evening's end, after we pulled into the driveway, Anna and Cal got out of the car and went inside the house, while Boyce and I, seemingly by mutual consent, remained in the car. We had not had a moment to ourselves all day, and this brief private time gave us an opportunity to express our feelings. I was so pleased when Boyce told me he wanted our relationship to continue — I felt exactly the same. I could see that he had enjoyed our time together as much as I.

Next morning Boyce returned to my friends' house, and we all took a long walk together along a creek in the woods — a perfect setting for picture-taking. Boyce had a camera, so I would have some pictures to show my secretary when I returned home. The day was fun! Later we parted long enough to dress for our dinner-theatre evening, and every moment after we were together again was just perfect. Around midnight we arrived back at Boyce's house, and he said that if I would like to stay a while, he would drive me back later. With my heart fluttering, I agreed.

His house was beautiful, decorated to perfection. Anna and Cal had told me that Boyce owned his own company and was now semi-retired. Clearly he had been extremely successful in business. My heart sank a little. Perhaps I wouldn't fit in. We were probably living in two separate worlds. Would this be a problem?

He showed me pictures of his wife, their two sons, and four grandchildren. In every nook and corner I could see the influence of a loving partner. We talked again about her and about his loss. I was truly sorry that he had lost her, yet I had to admit honestly that my own emotions were mixed. On the sympathy level, I wished that he still had his wife and that she could be around for her sons and grandchildren. But I was quickly coming to care for Boyce myself and greatly enjoying his company.

Yes, I still loved my husband's memory and always would, just as Boyce still loved and missed his wife. Nothing could change that for either of us. But I knew from experience that although one can learn to live with sorrow, it affords feeble nourishment for a lifetime.

The next morning I talked very frankly with Anna and Cal. I was troubled, because Boyce seemed to have so much more in a material way than I had ever been used to. They explained that he had grown up in humble circumstances but had built a very successful business. For many years they had considered him a workaholic. But now his son was running the business and Boyce was gradually stepping back. They also pointed out to me that if I was intimidated by Boyce's material success, he might be intimidated by my "degrees." This thought had never crossed my mind. Suddenly these no longer seemed like insurmountable obstacles.

After we had lunch together it was time for me to leave. The weekend had gone by in a flash and had been more fun than I had had at any time since Paul's death. Boyce and I were quickly becoming more than just friends.

And yet as I drove away that Sunday afternoon, with 150 miles to travel, I feared that the distance between us would limit our relationship. Boyce had told me that he suffered from narcolepsy — a sleep disorder — and that it would be dangerous for him to drive alone on trips. Perhaps I was an old-fashioned kind of woman, but I knew that for any relationship to work for me, I would have be the one being pursued. Time would tell.

Telling The News

When I arrived at home, my answering machine was bursting with messages. My two daughters, daughter-in-law, and secretary all wanted to know how the weekend had turned out. Before I had time even to return their calls, Boyce phoned to make sure that I had arrived safely. How thoughtful, and how nice! It had been a long time since anyone was concerned about my getting home. I had missed that, and it felt wonderfully warm and embracing to have it once again.

My family members seemed quite surprised by what I had to report. They were surprised, to begin with, that I actually liked this man. My teen-aged granddaughter asked what he looked like, and using language she understood, I said, "What a hunk!" She thought it was hilarious to hear Grandmommy talking like that. I could not disguise my energy and my excitement. Strangely, I had no anxiety about the eventual outcome. In this as in all else, I knew that God was utterly in control.

A few days later a package came from Boyce containing a gold shamrock charm for my bracelet. I had already given him the Blarney

Stone souvenir. Although I'm not a believer in "luck," for two sentimental people these were cherished reminders of a happy time — St. Patrick's Day, the day we first met.

Remembering the events of that weekend was a source of much pleasure to me and, sometimes, a smile. Since Boyce had been widowed only a few months, we had tried to be discreet about going to public places. I could understand his feelings about not wanting to be seen quite so soon with a woman companion in a town where he and his wife had had many friends. In spite of our caution, we had run into one couple whom he knew quite well, and I imagined they might be entertaining judgmental thoughts.

Well, it's easy to be judgmental when you don't understand the other person's circumstances. We who have lost a life partner don't always let other people know about it when we sit miserably at home, grieving, staring at emptiness, imagining we will never be happy again, recognizing that our families have their own lives to live and doing all we can to keep from being a problem for them.

The mere prospect of eating a meal alone is an unpleasant one, at least in the early stages of grief. Going alone to restaurants also depresses us at first. Boyce had all these feelings, yet the fact that he was able to enjoy the weekend certainly did not mean that he didn't still miss his wife. We never stop loving our partners who are gone.

I told no one other than my secretary about my trip to Atlanta. When I showed her the photographs we had taken, she was most impressed by this fine-looking man. Not knowing how the situation would unfold, I just felt it was in my best interest to keep quiet where other people were concerned. Was I in for a surprise!

Pursued

Returning to the office after a day of pastoral visits, I found a message taped to my door: "Boyce Jones called. Will call back tonight." Now I was curious. At the end of my work day I called Anna, asking if she knew why Boyce was calling. Her reply just bowled me over.

"He wants you to go to Las Vegas with us. We invited him to go, and he said that he would if you would go too."

Oh, my. These people had overlooked the fact that I had to work for a living, and I certainly didn't have the extra money for such a trip.

When Boyce called I was all prepared to tell him why I couldn't leave again so soon. Persistent, he told me that all I had to do was ask for the time off, because my expenses would all be paid. At that I concluded there would be no harm in asking, although I really didn't expect permission to take more vacation time just then.

When I spoke to my pastor, telling him some friends had invited me to go with them on an expense-paid trip to Las Vegas, I could hardly believe his reply: "You still have vacation time left. That's fine. Go on and have a good time!"

Emotions and questions whirled through my mind. I would have an opportunity to get to know Boyce better, and that would be good. Being with someone every day for a week will teach you a great deal about the person. But I knew too that it would be a week during which the relationship would either strengthen or die.

I was to fly to Atlanta and join Boyce to travel the rest of the way to Las Vegas, on April Fools' Day. Another omen? Cal and Anna would meet us there. With my heart beating fast and questions whirling in my head, I packed my bags and boarded the plane.

Boyce met me and suggested that we wait in the VIP lounge until our plane was ready for boarding. I had no idea what such a place might be like. It turned out to be a pleasant, comfortable waiting room with refreshments available — an "extra" that frequent flyers pay a yearly fee to make use of. That was my first "first."

The second "first" was that I had never before flown first class. That particular day, Cloud Nine must have been just outside the window beside my seat. God does give dessert! I could hardly believe I was traveling cross-country, first class, with a man I barely knew. Yet at the same time it seemed we had known each other for ages.

In Las Vegas we rented a car to drive to the hotel. The bellboy must have thought I was the most naïve woman in the West, for when he asked Boyce his name and Boyce replied, "Jones," the bellboy looked at me and said, "And I suppose your name is Smith." "No," I quickly replied, all innocence, "my name is Griz." Later Boyce explained the joke, and I was to have another reminder of it in the days ahead.

Many years before, I had spent just one night in Las Vegas, but the place had certainly changed. We spent hours walking around, taking in the sights. I couldn't believe this town. It was like a desert mirage! Huge lavish hotels were everywhere. Every block seemed to boast a wedding chapel. Having always thought Las Vegas was nothing but gambling games, I was surprised at how much else there was to see and do. When we came upon a wishing well, we stopped and both made a wish — two identical wishes that were destined to come true.

After Anna and Cal arrived, we took in the first of many night-time shows. In the daytime we went sightseeing, and, yes, even tried our luck at the slot machines. Before the week was over, Boyce and I had become more than just friends — we were engaged.

The Miracle Business

Years before, I had made that list of all the qualities that I would desire in a man in order to give serious thought to marrying again. Boyce had every one, plus some others I hadn't even thought about. At that point I had been a widow for 13 years. Now I had no doubts that God's plan was for me to marry Boyce. I had said so many times that if I ever found someone I could love, it would be a miracle from God. All I can say is that God is still in the miracle business.

Why were Anna and Cal so surprised when we told them of our decision? Perhaps they thought we were rushing things, and no doubt they felt somewhat responsible. But Boyce and I had no doubts.

I knew that Boyce still had grieving to do, and I understood that because I had been through it myself. Healing would take time, and I intended to allow him as much time as he needed and be there for him all the way. Not everyone could have handled this situation, but I believed that with empathy, understanding, and God's ever-present grace, I could make a pretty good try.

Love With All The Trimmings

We took the red-eye flight back to Atlanta, and immediately Boyce and I went shopping for a diamond ring. My sense of humor came to the rescue when the long overnight flight and Boyce's narcolepsy caused him to fall asleep at the jewelry-store counter. The sales assistant must have thought that Boyce had no interest whatever in being engaged to be married. After the decision was made, I told Boyce that I had picked out a really big diamond while he dozed. Later that day Boyce arranged for me to meet one of his sons, a daughter-in-law, and grandchildren. All were friendly and pleasant and managed to disguise whatever surprise and curiosity they must have felt.

When I returned to South Carolina I called my pastor and finally shared my good news. After he got over his surprise, he asked if he could make it public. Of course now I wanted everyone to know. The next morning during the worship service when he invited me to stand beside him as he told the congregation, a loud collective gasp was heard. No one had known that I was interested in anyone or dating at all.

On Monday at our staff meeting, some of those who hadn't heard the announcement accused me of wearing a fake engagement ring as a joke. Even so, everyone was very happy for me. Boyce and I had just about decided that we would set a date in May for our wedding.

The next weekend was Easter, and Boyce flew down to see me, checking into a nearby hotel. On Friday evening we attended a musical program at the church, and when we walked in, an entire row of senior adults turned around in unison to size up this man who was marrying their Jane. I'm sure we were the topic of fevered conversation. Boyce took the attention in good spirits and seemed to enjoy the weekend. I certainly did, and I was more than proud to introduce him to my friends.

My own family and out-of-town friends were also very happy to hear of my engagement, even though they had not yet met Boyce. My children just said, "Mom, it's fine. We're happy for you. We know you know what you're doing."

I was beginning to wonder how we would ever arrange a May wedding, because the month was a very busy one in my job. At that time of year we always had our Senior Adult Celebration including special programs, a banquet and special recognitions, and leadership of a Sunday evening service, all requiring much preparation.

Also on the May calendar was a Sunday School class retreat at Callaway Gardens in Pine Mountain, Georgia, where Boyce owned a cottage. Boyce's class had invited me to take part. Anna and Cal, Boyce and I would be staying there together. Of course by now Boyce's closest friends knew of our engagement, and I was looking forward to this outing where we would no longer have to worry about "being seen."

Casseroles Versus Convertibles

As we talked about our coming marriage plans, Boyce enjoyed telling me about his conversation after his wife's death with a widowed friend who had eventually married again. Knowing that some unattached women are quick to set their caps for any available man, this friend had warned him, "Beware of women coming to the house with casseroles!" After meeting me, Boyce told his friend she had left out the most important warning: "Beware of a blonde in a convertible!"

A Spring Wedding

During April, on one of several visits I made to Atlanta, Boyce suggested we go ahead and get our marriage license. This man always plans ahead. When we went to the courthouse, I felt rather awkward, especially when I had to give my age. Later the same day we looked at new convertibles, for Boyce wanted to give me one for a wedding gift. After all my years of sadness, confusion, and bewilderment, these were great days. Our brief times together were wonderful, and after I returned home we talked on the phone every night.

My senior adults wanted to know when we would be married. Some time in May, I said, although no date had been set. In any case, we had decided to make it a very private affair.

At first I wanted to put off our wedding until after the Senior Adult Celebration, so that my heaviest church responsibilities would be out of the way. But Boyce wanted us to marry sooner than that. I was trying to think how it would all work out, for I didn't want us to marry and then have to part for several weeks. Eventually he persuaded me to change my mind. At our age, it didn't make sense to waste precious time.

During these exciting days of looking forward to our marriage we had two very special songs: "Keeper of the Stars" and "The Second Time Around." Both truly expressed how we felt about our love for each other.

The Second Time Around

We had some essential paperwork to take care of first. As we both had grown children — Boyce had two and I had three — we thought it sensible to have a prenuptial agreement. I wanted no misunderstandings, and Boyce felt the same. There was no lack of trust, just good common sense. Boyce had his papers ready, but I had not had time to consult with an attorney yet.

We had already chosen Tom, Boyce's friend who had been an associate pastor on the church staff, to marry us, and because he would be attending the retreat at Callaway too, we began to think of getting married in the Callaway Gardens chapel. My lawyer wasn't sure he could have my papers ready in time, but he would try. I didn't mention to anyone else the possible wedding date. My friends knew I was going on the retreat but didn't suspect other plans. When I packed my bag, I put in a new dress that I could wear for our wedding, just in case.

Before we left, Boyce took me to have lunch with his sister and the son I hadn't met. Naturally, I was nervous, wondering what they would think of me. Southern folk have good manners, though, and both were cordial to me during the pleasant meal. I knew the circumstances must be difficult for them. Boyce's sister did comment that she didn't know why we had to be in such a hurry. I could understand; sisters are protective.

That afternoon when I met with my attorney alone to go over the prenuptial agreement, I began losing my voice. I was embarrassed. Was I allergic to something in the office, or allergic to the prospect of marriage? He still couldn't promise to have the papers ready the next day when we were to leave for Callaway.

That evening we had dinner with some of Boyce's closest friends — again, all extremely friendly and nice. I felt welcomed and accepted, even though I could scarcely speak. They must have wondered what had happened to my voice. And in addition to losing my voice, I had begun breaking out in a rash. What in the world was wrong with me? First my voice, and then my skin, and the uncertainty of the prenuptial agreement being ready — all these things were doubtless affecting my nerves.

Next morning the lawyer called. The papers were ready! We could get married! My voice improved, and my rash went away. I was as nearly normal as could be hoped for. The date was May 5, 1995, and I was 65 — nine months older than Boyce, a fact that delights him.

The Perfect Place

At Callaway I saw Boyce's cottage for the first time — our honeymoon cottage — to be shared with Anna and Cal. Fortunately each couple would have plenty of privacy. Thoughtful Boyce had five gorgeous pink roses waiting for me, to carry as my bridal bouquet.

A picturesque vacation resort known for its flowers, dogwood trees, and azaleas, Callaway Gardens is gloriously beautiful in the spring. Its small chapel features stained-glass windows for the four seasons of the year, and a large lake mirrors its reflection — a quaint and beautiful sight, a favorite picture-taking spot.

The other retreat-goers weren't arriving until dinnertime, so we had plenty of time to follow through with our plans. Slipping into the chapel with our pastor friend Tom, his wife Sue, and Cal and Anna as our witnesses, Boyce and I were married at five minutes past five. During our wedding, a tourist stopped by to take a video, and ever since then I've wondered whose vacation video features the wedding of the mystery couple — Jane and Boyce Jones.

After taking our own pictures, we joined the rest of our group for a buffet dinner. How surprised everyone was when Boyce announced that we were newlyweds. The Sunday School class had already planned a little engagement party for us, with cake and punch. We turned it into a wedding celebration.

United In Faith

Boyce and I had no doubts about our seemingly hasty wedding. We were blissfully happy. God had been so good to us! We both "knew" that God had been the instigator, and all was His plan for our lives at this time. It is such a joy when your partner shares your deep-rooted faith. It makes all the difference in how the two of you approach life and the many challenges that come.

Over the weekend we withstood the usual teasing in good humor. While the other men played golf and the other women shopped, Boyce and I took pictures and walked the nature trails, glorying in the beauty of the place. That night Boyce called his family to tell them of our marriage. On Sunday afternoon, with the weekend nearly at an end, I called my own children.

Parting, at least for a time, was inevitable. When I boarded the plane for South Carolina still carrying my bridal flowers, someone said, "You must have been a bridesmaid in someone's wedding."

"No," I replied, "I was the bride."

Did she look startled! "What happened to the groom?" was the next question, and my questioner seemed even more puzzled when

I told her he couldn't come with me at this time. The country wasn't at war. Maybe she thought he was in jail!

Returning to work on Monday morning, after our usual staff meeting I placed my wedding pictures on the table. "When you're as old we are," I said with a smile, "you can't afford to waste time." Boyce and I had met on March 17 and married on May 5.

Later one of the younger associate pastors told me privately, "I just loved hearing you say that you and Boyce couldn't wait to get married. That gives us all hope!" I took it as I believe he meant it — that God gives us the ability to love and share our lives with someone special, that a God-given opportunity to recapture the full experience of love is wonderful at any age.

Adjustments Begin

My plan was to retire a few weeks later. Meanwhile I was to make a flying trip to spend a weekend with Boyce at his house; I knew Anna and Cal were glad their houseguest had finally made some other arrangements. However, I still found it difficult to realize that I was truly married.

I called Boyce before heading for Atlanta. "I've found out I'll be able to stay an extra night," I told him. "Will that be all right?"

He burst out laughing. "You're asking your husband for permission to stay an extra night? I'll check my schedule to be sure."

After that weekend with Boyce I found it doubly hard to return to work, knowing I would not be seeing him for two more weeks. Yet Boyce had a major challenge ahead. Before I could come to live in his house, he would need to empty closets and remove clothes that had belonged to his wife. Personal items and things in dresser drawers had to be dealt with. This process is painful, because it involves closure. Memories of the happy past surface and sometimes don't want to be dismissed. I just prayed that God would fill Boyce's need at this difficult time.

Fortunately, friends and family rallied to help. He gave away many of his wife's things to her close friends, just as I had done with Paul's things many years before. There is comfort in knowing that we are doing as they would want us to do.

Since Boyce's house was filled with everything necessary for comfortable living, I decided to give most of my furniture to my children, keeping only items with sentimental value. I would move just two pieces of my own: a small desk and my organ. My children would pick up everything else, keeping what they wanted and holding a garage sale to dispose of the rest.

Rituals of Remembrance

Boyce and I both wanted to keep fresh flowers on our spouses' graves at the appropriate times. We still do that. I also knew that at times he would want to go by the cemetery, alone, and I knew that holidays and particular dates would sadden him. You don't forget decades of happy marriage in a few short months. None of this would I have understood had I not gone through the process myself. For Boyce, it was not yet time to close the door on the past.

During the time that we were apart, Boyce sent another dozen red roses to my office. If men only knew how much this gesture means to us women, they would all send flowers to wives or girl-friends on the slightest excuse. Yes, a dozen red roses may be costly, but a single flower in a vase carries a message of love as well. All his thoughtful gestures and gifts endeared him to me so much. I felt continually thankful that God had brought us together.

When my new husband inquired about a greeting card he had sent, I had to tell him that I hadn't received it. Then he told me that as a joke, he had addressed it to Jane Smith, recalling the incident of Jones and Smith at the hotel in Las Vegas. I told him that in the small town where I lived, the mailman knew everybody, and he knew that I wasn't Jane Smith.

A week later the card was delivered to me, with another person's writing on the envelope: "Opened by mistake." We hoped Boyce hadn't got somebody else in trouble, for the card's message was simply, "Thank you for a great weekend."

Boyce came to be with me on my last weekend at my church job, along with Anna and Cal. The church gave us a beautiful reception, even including a wedding cake. It was a wonderful send-off. With very mixed feelings, I managed to pack and label things from my office. I had had a good four years here, and I knew I would miss the people. The staff had even given me a lingerie shower after my wedding. I appreciated all these expressions of love and caring. God had blessed me so much in providing this job for me and these wonderful working relationships. Now I wondered what His plan for my future would be, as Boyce's wife.

Here Comes The Bride

My daughter Melanie and her husband Mike were to fly in in order to help me move. Through a peculiar matter of pride on my part, I sent Boyce, Anna and Cal back to Atlanta, for I wanted to take care of all my responsibilities myself. I even insisted on paying my own moving expenses. I did not want anyone to imagine that I expected Boyce to meet my obligations. I had already paid all my bills to spare him that unpleasant surprise. I didn't want the slightest hint that I might have married because of money, and I trusted that anyone who knew me well would know it couldn't be so.

Melanie and Mike were downcast when they arrived to see how little packing I had been able to do. Things had simply been happening too fast! Fortunately, several good church friends came and worked all day, helping us pack and load the rental truck. Melanie and I are still greatly indebted to them. My only excuse was that my own personal "Cloud Nine" had been floating so high and so wide, I just couldn't get everything done. And Boyce and I were to leave on our honeymoon just a few days after my belongings and I arrived in Atlanta.

When we drove up to Boyce's house, a shiny new red convertible was parked in the yard, decorated with balloons saying "Welcome Home." Throughout the house more balloons were strung, with such merry messages as "Happy Retirement" and "Never Too Old To Party" — my favorite. The stereo was playing beautiful music. With Melanie and Mike meeting Boyce for the first time, I quickly saw that they liked him very much. Whew! After helping me unload my boxes of books, pictures, and mementos, and moving my organ and desk into the sitting area of the bedroom, they were on their way back to Tennessee. It was a happy time.

Time For Each Other

Two days later we headed for a Florida honeymoon. Strange thoughts still haunted me from time to time as I thought about the two weeks ahead. What will we talk about? It sounds crazy, but we still did not know each other well enough for me to have an answer to such a question. And never mind about two weeks — what about the rest of our lives? Would we be as happy as I imagined? When these uncertainties arose, I just turned them over to God, confident that He hadn't brought me this far to disappoint me now.

We stopped in Key Largo to visit Lu Ann, my other daughter, and give her a chance to meet Boyce, then continued to Key West, where we had a great time. In this delightful town where the air was fresh with the salty savor of the sea, I remembered that one of our wedding gifts had been a plaque with the following words:

"May there be such a oneness between you in your marriage
That when one of you weeps, the other will taste salt."

I prayed to know that oneness. Every indication was that it would be so.

The only one of my children who had not yet met Boyce was my son, and we planned to travel to his area in the summer. No doubt he and his sisters did much talking on the phone about their mom and her new husband after those first meetings.

Were there adjustments for Boyce and me the second time around? Oh, there were adjustments. Even so, we were happy and compatible. I believe this was because both of us are reasonably flexible people, generally optimistic, who want to repeat the happiness of our first marriages. We both knew that some compromises would have to be made, and we have made them cheerfully.

Trusting To Time

If I had asked him to do so, Boyce would have sold his lovely house, but I knew he wasn't yet ready. I just moved in, changing nothing. Everything remained as it had been. The place didn't feel like home to me — not a home that I had had the pleasure of creating — but I understood that Boyce had a process to work through, and I didn't want to short-circuit that process. When I found myself speaking of "Boyce's house," I realized that someday we would live in a place I could call "our house."

Boyce's family members were always accepting of me and kind, even though they were still mourning the loss of a mother and a grandmother. The four grandchildren were precious, and I loved them instantly. I knew better than to try to take their grandmother's place, for she was very special to them. I just wanted to be their friend and have us get to know each other.

Children have a wonderful way of getting right to the truth of things. One day after they had been visiting us, as their mother was driving them home, the youngest boy wanted to know exactly

111

who I was. His mother told him that I was his step-grandmother.
"What's a step-grandmother?" he asked.

All of these children participated in a community softball program,
and his older brother had the perfect answer: "She's a back-up."

No more questions!

Attending Boyce's church was difficult for me. Even though
people were cordial there too, I felt like an intruder. They had all
known and liked June, Boyce's first wife. Anna and Cal were the
only people in that congregation whom I could consider "my" friends,
although Tom, who had performed our wedding ceremony, and his
wife Sue were thoughtful of me.

Comparisons

If you marry again you must accept certain things. One is the
inevitability of comparisons. I was totally different from Boyce's
first wife, who had been very athletic, good at all sports, and loved
to entertain, decorate the house, and shop at garage sales. Comparisons are understandable, but every single one of us has the right to
be an individual. I had to be me — Jane. I could not be a clone of
the wife who was gone.

Boyce was also utterly different from my first husband, but because
I had moved into his neighborhood and his circle of acquaintances,
there was no one around to make a comparison between him and
Paul. Thank goodness! It certainly made Boyce's life easier, not being
told all the time how different my two husbands were.

Boyce and his wife had always bowled on the church bowling
team. I didn't know one thing about bowling, but I knew that I had
better figure out a way to fit in. I got myself fitted with a bowling
ball and bowling shoes, and I took some bowling lessons. If this
activity was important to Boyce, I was determined to make it important to me as well. In the course of this bowling involvement I met
some very congenial people, but in all honesty I never improved
much on my game. Boyce was accepting about that, yet I couldn't
help wondering if he was embarrassed that his new wife couldn't
measure up in the bowling department.

Sadness Lingers

During our first few months of marriage, some times were very
difficult for Boyce. Late one evening as he was working in his office,

I went on to bed, but I couldn't go to sleep, because I heard him weeping. I imagined that he was writing in his journal, which was a good way to express his feelings. I called to him, asking if he was all right, and he assured me that he was.

I just had to let him feel his feelings and express them in whatever way was helpful and comforting. I knew he could only move beyond his sadness by working his way through it. Had I said, "Oh, Boyce, don't feel sad!" and tried to jolly him out of those sad feelings, I would have invalidated his need to mourn and burdened him further with the effort of trying not feel his grief. Life is not like that. As the writer of Ecclesiastes so wisely observed, *"There is a time for tears, a time for laughter; a time for mourning, a time for dancing."* Our times of laughter and dancing would return.

Once in a while I even wished that Boyce had not lost his wife, and that I had never met him. Does that sound strange? I was entering into his feelings of loss myself. When we attended the grandchildren's sporting events, I wished that their grandmother could have been there. I told Boyce these feelings, and he appreciated them. We truly loved each other, and true love takes understanding.

In addition, I knew that Boyce's feelings about losing his first wife didn't mean that he loved me any less. Nor had I forgotten about the man I had been married to for 33 years. I had room in my heart to love Boyce, too, just as he had room to love me.

Filling The Days

Fortunately, during those early months, God gave me time to adjust to my new situation. I didn't rush things. I just took the new life one day at a time, remembering that every day was a gift and finding the good in each one. Boyce was then working three days a week at his company, so I had time to fill. I got busy writing some articles on senior adult work for a denominational magazine, and since I was no longer teaching a class or involved in local church work, I had time to enjoy shopping, reading, and playing my organ.

I still felt like an intruder of sorts in this house. I hesitated to open drawers or look through anything, for everything belonged to someone else. True, I had carved out my little corner of our bedroom. Otherwise everything was as it had been before I came.

I tell these things only to emphasize that adjustments and growth are essential in any marriage. Yet Boyce and I were very happy. He was so attentive! I still was surprised by gifts of roses on special occasions, and he was extremely generous and good to my family. We were enjoying life and having fun, but as the months passed, Boyce's grief was no longer so fresh, and I knew that the time was drawing near when we could make a change — moving to a new house that would belong to us both.

A New Nest

When Boyce retired altogether, we began thinking about where we would like to live. We considered Florida but decided against it when we remembered how far we would be from our families. Next we thought of moving to a place on the lake. Both of us loved the water and all of nature, and lake homes were available about 50 miles from where we were then living. When the couple we had run into on our first date (when we were hoping nobody would see us together) told us of a nice house for sale, we decided to see the place for ourselves.

Set on a little rise above the lake shore, the house was beautiful, and it had a boat dock. Boyce and I knew right away that this was the place for us. We made the owner an offer and put the old house on the market. We were so excited! When our offer was accepted, we bought everything new for the main level of the new house and began staying there most of the time, even though the old house didn't sell immediately. Now I was finally at home.

Wanting our families to be able to visit and enjoy the lake, we bought a boat and a Wave-Runner™. Boyce began doing the yard work, and we planted flowers. Fortunate in having good neighbors, we were also just about two miles from a huge outlet mall — a shopper's paradise. We had all the conveniences of a town combined with the wonderful, peaceful atmosphere of living on the lake.

The other house took nine months to sell, and that was good, because when the time came to have a garage sale and sell furniture, Boyce was emotionally and mentally ready. He could move on.

As I conclude my story, Boyce and I have been happily married for four years. After moving, we joined a church where neither of us knew anyone and have made new friends there together. We had a wonderful trip to Hawaii, and we still do some traveling with

114

friends. Life has been very good. Our families visit and enjoy the lake, happy for our happiness and relieved that they don't have to worry about us.

Each morning as we look out over the deck to the beautiful lake view, watching the squirrels playfully seeking a handout, listening to the birds sing and chatter, we share an embrace and thank God for all that He has given us. We have both been on the journey from grief to gladness, and God has supplied every need, each step of the way. We give Him all the glory!

> *"I will sing of the Lord's great love forever;*
> *With my mouth I will make your faithfulness known."*
>
> — *Psalm 89:1*

Postscript

Jane's Recipe For Living Well

When my father died, my 62-year-old mother, who had taken an active role in the family business up to that point, suddenly became dependent and seemingly helpless. For whatever reason, she refused to help herself. Although she had been an extremely competent woman, at that point in her life she began dwelling ceaselessly on her situation, felt sorry for herself, and was constantly unhappy. She expected too much of family members and friends. Because she was so miserable, no one wanted to be around her for very long. We loved her, but we couldn't understand or appreciate her refusal to try to make it on her own and have a meaningful life in the years that remained to her. What a tragic waste. And when I became a widow, my mother's sad example stood before me as the way I did not want to choose.

After writing about my own journey from grief to gladness, I reflected on how I was able to build a good new life. My suggestions — I call them my Recipe For Living Well — may also speak to you. Whatever the situation may be that you are hoping to move beyond in order to discover the new thing God has in store for you, I hope you will also find your own Recipe for Living Well.

Willingness: Being willing to accept opportunities that came my way, even though many times they were not what I would have wanted or expected at that stage of life. For example, when I enrolled in seminary, I certainly never expected to be working on a riverboat — yet God had a purpose for me there. What opportunity may be waiting for you, what place where God can use you?

Attitude: I couldn't always help what happened to me, but I could help what happened *within me*. Instead of fretting about my limitations, I could choose to bloom where I was planted. I could be miserable, or I could trust that God had new gifts in store for me.

Goals: By making plans and doing all within my power to work with the help of God to accomplish them, I found meaning in life. Instead of simply reacting to circumstances, I did my best to set goals and take some small step every day toward those goals.

Faith: Countless times, I had questions that remained unanswered. During these times of uncertainty, I had to accept what I could not change, make the best effort I could, and move forward, trusting God for the outcome. If faith does not come easy for you, just fake it until you make it. Acting "as if" can create new realities.

Humor: Surely God has a sense of humor — just look at the human beings He created! Being able to laugh freely and spontaneously was probably the most important thing I could do to help myself. I soon learned that people want to be around cheerful people, not gloomy ones. I look for something to laugh at every day and resist the temptation to take myself too seriously.

Persistence: Giving myself permission to go on living and loving, without guilt, was vital. My first husband would not have wanted to see me become petrified in my grief and loss. I don't believe God wants us to do that either. If we do our part and keep on keeping on, we will discover many of the deepest satisfactions of life.

118

Jane does her senior-banquet thing.

Number One Senior-In-Denial

Jane and Boyce on their wedding day

Still having fun!

Jane Jones is available for seminars and talks on the following topics:

Rediscovering The Joys Of Life After A Personal Loss

Life Really Begins At 60!

She may be reached at:

360 Browns Point
Dawsonville, GA 30534

Phone (706) 216-4559
FAX (706) 216-4561

Additional copies of this book are available from the author.

To order, copy and fill in the order blank and mail it with your check.

Name: _____

Address: _____

City: _____ State: _____ Zip: _____

Phone: (_____) _____
        AREA CODE

_____ Copies × $12.95 per copy =   _____

Add for shipping & handling $ 2.95

TOTAL   _____

**Mail order with
check payable to Jane G. Jones to:**

Jane Griz Jones
360 Browns Point
Dawsonville, GA 30534

Recovery Communications, Inc.

BOOK PUBLISHING & AUTHOR PROMOTIONS
Post Office Box 19910 • Baltimore, Maryland 21211, USA

Now available through your local bookstore!

Jennifer J. Richardson, M.S.W. *Diary of Abuse/Diary of Healing.* A young girl's secret journal recording two decades of abuse, with detailed healing therapy sessions. A raw and extraordinary book that will inspire other abuse survivors with new hope. **Contact the author at (404) 373-1837.**

Toby Rice Drews. *Getting Them Sober, Volume One — You Can Help!* Hundreds of ideas for sobriety and recovery. The million-seller endorsed by Melody Beattie, Dr. Norman Vincent Peale, and "Dear Abby." **Contact the author at (410) 243-8352.**

Toby Rice Drews. *Getting Them Sober, Volume Four — Separation Decisions.* All about detachment, separation, and child custody issues for families of alcoholics. A "book of immense value," says Max Weisman, M.D., past president of the American Society of Addiction Medicine. **Contact the author at (410) 243-8352.**

Betsy Tice White. *Turning Your Teen Around: How A Couple Helped Their Troubled Son While Keeping Their Marriage Alive and Well.* A doctor family's successful personal battle against teen-age drug use, with powerfully helpful tips for parents in pain. Endorsed by John Palmer, former news anchor, NBC's TODAY Show. **Contact the author at (770) 590-7311.**

Betsy Tice White. *Mountain Folk/Mountain Food: Down-Home Wisdom, Plain Tales, and Recipe Secrets from Appalachia.* The joy of living as expressed in delightful vignettes and mouth-watering regional foods. Endorsed by the Discovery Channel's "Great Country Inns" and *Blue Ridge Country Magazine.* **Contact the author at (770) 590-7311.**

Linda Meyer, Ph.D. *I See Myself Changing: Weekly Meditations and Recovery Journaling for Young Adults.* A life-affirming book for adolescents and young adults, endorsed by Robert Bulkeley of The Gilman School. **Contact the author at (217) 367-8821.**

Mattie Carroll Mullins. *JUDY: The Murder of My Daughter, The Healing of My Family.* A Christian mother's inspiring story of how her family moved from unimaginable tragedy to forgiveness. **Contact the author at (423) 926-7827.**

Joseph C. Buccilli, Ph.D. *Wise Stuff About Relationships: Spiritual Reflections and Recovery Journal.* A gem of a book for anyone in recovery; "an empowering spiritual workout." Endorsed by the vice-president of the *Philadelphia Inquirer.* **Contact the author at (609) 629-4441.**

Stacie Hagan and Charlie Palmgren. *The Chicken Conspiracy: Breaking the Cycle of Personal Stress and Organizational Mediocrity.* A liberating message from corporate trainers about successful personal, organizational, and global change. **Contact the authors at (404) 297-9388.**

David E. Bergesen. *Murder Crosses the Equator: A Father Jack Carthier Mystery.* Volcanic tale of suspense in a Latin-American setting, starring a clever missionary-priest detective. **Contact the author at (520) 744-2631.**

John Pearson. *Eastern Shore Beckonings.* Marvelous trek back in time through charming villages and encounters with solid Chesapeake Bay folk. "Aches with affection" — The *Village Voice's* Washington correspondent. **Contact the author at (410) 315-7940.**

Jerry Zeller. *The Shaman and Other Almost-Tall Tales.* The enchantment of story-telling and grace-filled character sketches from an Episcopal archdeacon and former Emory University Dean. **Contact the author at (706) 692-5842.**

AND COMING SOON . . .

Linda Meyer, Ph.D. *Why Is It So Hard To Take Care Of My Parent?* The only book that deals head-on with the nitty-gritty of eldercare issues in dysfunctional families.

Miles A. Moody. *The Cliff Birds.* Brilliantly alive with the veterinarian-author's vivid illustrations, this self-discovery fable, starring a confused parrot, speaks movingly to older children and truth-seeking adults alike.

Mattie Carroll Mullins. *Preachers' Wives Tell All! Lively Tales and Tasty Recipes from Country Parsonage Kitchens.* The lighter side of life from the point of view of the pastor's helpmate, with plenty of appetizing recipes thrown in.